Business Bank Statement Mortgage Loans

How to Use Business Revenue to Qualify for a Mortgage Loan

By Joseph G. Correa

Licensed Mortgage Broker, Finibi Mortgage

Copyright & Legal Notice

Published by Live Stronger Faster

The information provided in this book is for educational and informational purposes only and does not constitute financial, legal, tax, or investment advice. Although the author is a licensed mortgage professional, the content presented is general in nature and is not intended as personalized guidance for any specific individual or financial situation.

The strategies, structuring methods, and examples discussed in this book are illustrative and educational in nature. They are intended to demonstrate concepts related to bank statement mortgage loan qualification and structuring, including deposit analysis, expense ratio application, and investor guideline interpretation. These examples do not represent guaranteed outcomes or approvals. Results may vary significantly based on individual financial profiles, documentation, credit history, property type, and lender-specific requirements.

The author and publisher make no representations or warranties regarding the accuracy, completeness, or applicability of the content and disclaim any liability for errors, omissions, or outcomes resulting from the use or misuse of the information contained in this book.

All trademarks, service marks, company names, and product names referenced in this publication are the property of their respective owners and are used strictly for identification and educational purposes only. Their inclusion does not imply endorsement or affiliation.

First Edition, 2026

Table of Contents

Introduction

In today's evolving lending environment, the traditional rules of mortgage qualification are no longer the only path to homeownership or real estate investment. For decades, borrowers were expected to present tax returns that clearly documented income, stability, and ability to repay. But what happens when those tax returns do not accurately reflect the true financial strength of a borrower? What happens when a successful business owner shows minimal taxable income due to legitimate deductions, reinvestment strategies, or aggressive tax planning? This is where business bank statement mortgage loans emerge as one of the most powerful and flexible tools available in modern lending.

This book is designed to give you a complete, strategic understanding of how to use business revenue—not just reported income—to qualify for a mortgage loan. Whether you are a self-employed entrepreneur, a business owner with multiple revenue streams, or an investor scaling operations across different entities, the ability to leverage your business bank statements can open doors that traditional underwriting would otherwise keep closed. The goal of this introduction is to shift your mindset from thinking like a traditional borrower to thinking like a strategic borrower—someone who understands how lenders evaluate cash flow, risk, and opportunity.

One of the biggest misconceptions in mortgage lending is that income equals what is reported on tax returns. In reality, especially for business owners, income is often far more complex. A business may generate significant gross revenue, but after expenses, depreciation, and write-offs, the taxable income may appear minimal. While this is beneficial for tax purposes, it can create challenges when applying for a conventional loan. Business bank statement loans solve this problem by focusing on cash flow rather than tax-adjusted income. Instead of asking, "What did you report?" lenders ask, "What is actually flowing through your accounts?"

This shift is critical. It changes the entire approach to qualification. Instead of being penalized for maximizing deductions, borrowers can now be evaluated based on the strength of their business operations. Deposits become the foundation of income analysis. Patterns of revenue become more important than line items on a tax return. Consistency, stability, and scalability of business income take center stage. As you progress through this book, you will learn how underwriters interpret these patterns and how to position your financial profile to align with their expectations. Another key concept introduced in this book is the difference between revenue and profit. Many borrowers assume that lenders will simply use total deposits as qualifying income, but that is not the case. Lenders recognize that businesses have expenses, and they apply what is known as an expense ratio to determine usable income. This ratio varies depending on the type of business, industry standards, and documentation provided. In some cases, a fixed expense factor is applied—such as 50%—to estimate net income. In other cases, a CPA-prepared profit and loss statement can be used to justify a lower expense ratio, increasing the borrower's qualifying income.

Understanding how to navigate this distinction between revenue and profit is one of the most important skills you will develop. It is not just about how much money your business makes; it is about how that money is structured, documented, and presented. Two borrowers with identical revenue can qualify for dramatically different loan amounts depending on how their financials are organized. This is where strategy becomes essential. This is where knowledge becomes leverage.

The use of CPA-prepared profit and loss statements adds another layer of sophistication to the process. When properly prepared, these documents can validate lower expense ratios and provide a clearer picture of business profitability. However, they must align with bank statements and demonstrate consistency. Underwriters are trained to identify discrepancies, and any mismatch between reported figures and actual deposits can raise red flags. This book will guide you through how to properly use CPA documentation to strengthen your file rather than complicate it.

In addition to understanding income calculations, you will also learn how lenders evaluate the overall strength of a business. It is not enough to show deposits; those deposits must make sense. They must be consistent over time. They must align with the nature of the business. Seasonal fluctuations, irregular spikes, and unexplained variances can all impact how income is perceived. By learning how to identify and manage these factors, you can proactively address potential concerns before they become obstacles in underwriting.

Another important aspect of business bank statement loans is the type of business structure you operate under. Whether you are a sole proprietor, an LLC, an S corporation, or a partnership, each structure has implications for how income is analyzed. Some structures allow for simpler documentation, while others require additional layers of verification. Understanding how your business structure affects your loan application will help you make more informed decisions not only about financing but also about how you operate your business moving forward.

This book also emphasizes the importance of clean and organized financial accounts. One of the most common mistakes borrowers make is mixing personal and business finances. This creates confusion, complicates underwriting, and can lead to reduced qualifying income. By maintaining clear separation between business and personal accounts, you create a more transparent financial profile that is easier for lenders to evaluate. Clean accounts lead to stronger files. Stronger files lead to better approvals.

As you move deeper into this book, you will begin to see that qualifying for a mortgage using business bank statements is not just about meeting requirements—it is about engineering your approval. It is about understanding the rules well enough to work within them strategically. It is about positioning your financial profile in a way that highlights strengths and minimizes weaknesses. This is the difference between hoping for approval and controlling the outcome.

The concept of expense ratio strategies is particularly powerful in this regard. By understanding how different lenders apply expense factors, you can choose programs that align with your business model. Some industries naturally have lower expenses, while others operate on thinner margins. Knowing how to match your business to the right lender can significantly increase your qualifying income and expand your financing options. This is not guesswork; it is a calculated approach to loan structuring. It is also important to recognize that not all deposits are treated equally. Lenders will distinguish between eligible and ineligible income sources. Transfers between accounts, one-time deposits, and non-business-related income may be excluded from calculations. This makes it essential to understand how to present your deposits in a way that clearly reflects business activity. Proper documentation and explanation can make the difference between including or excluding significant portions of your income.

Throughout this book, you will also gain insight into the mindset of underwriters. Understanding how they think, what they look for, and how they assess risk will give you a significant advantage. Underwriters are not just reviewing numbers; they are telling a story about your financial profile. Your goal is to make that story clear, consistent, and compelling. When your file tells a strong story, approvals become smoother and faster.

Another powerful takeaway from this book is the realization that business bank statement loans are not just a workaround—they are a legitimate and strategic financing solution. As the economy continues to shift toward entrepreneurship, gig work, and self-employment, these loan programs are becoming increasingly mainstream. Lenders recognize that traditional income documentation does not capture the full picture for modern borrowers. By embracing alternative documentation, they are expanding access to financing in a way that reflects how people actually earn money today.

This book is not just about getting approved for one loan. It is about building a long-term strategy for financing your goals. Whether you are purchasing a primary residence, investing in rental properties, or scaling a real estate portfolio, the principles you learn here can be applied repeatedly. Once you understand how to structure your income, manage your accounts, and present your financial profile, you can use these strategies to unlock ongoing opportunities.

You will also begin to see how business bank statement loans can be combined with other financing strategies. For example, pairing bank statement income with investment property cash flow, or using these loans in conjunction with DSCR programs, can create powerful leverage. The more you understand the tools available to you, the more creative and effective your financing strategies can become.

As you continue through this series, each book will build on the foundation established here. Book 1 introduced the fundamentals. Book 2 focused on personal bank statements. Now, in Book 3, we are taking a deeper dive into the business side of income analysis. This is where complexity increases, but so does opportunity. Mastering business bank statement loans puts you in a position to operate at a higher level—one where you are not limited by traditional rules but empowered by strategic knowledge.

By the time you finish this book, you will have a clear understanding of how to calculate qualifying income using business bank statements, how to leverage CPA-prepared documentation, how to apply expense ratio strategies, and how to structure your financial profile for maximum approval potential. More importantly, you will have the confidence to navigate the process with clarity and control.

The path to approval is no longer limited to what you report on paper. It is defined by what you can prove through your business activity, your consistency, and your strategy. This book will show you how to turn your business revenue into a powerful tool for achieving your real estate and financial goals.

Chapter 1

Understanding Business Bank Statement Income and How Lenders Evaluate Revenue

When it comes to qualifying for a mortgage using business bank statements, the most important concept to understand is that lenders are no longer focused on what you report on your tax returns—they are focused on what your business actually generates in real cash flow. This shift changes everything. Instead of relying on adjusted income after deductions, lenders analyze the raw deposits flowing into your business accounts and then apply structured methods to determine how much of that income can be used to qualify you for a loan. This chapter is designed to help you fully understand how that process works, how lenders think, and how you can position your business income to maximize your approval potential.

At the core of business bank statement lending is the concept of deposit-based income analysis. Lenders typically review 12 or 24 months of business bank statements to identify patterns of revenue. They are not just looking at totals—they are analyzing consistency, trends, and the nature of the deposits. Regular deposits that align with the type of business you operate are considered strong indicators of stable income. For example, if you own a consulting firm and consistently receive client payments on a weekly or monthly basis, those deposits help build a predictable income profile. On the other hand, large irregular deposits without explanation may raise questions and require further documentation.

One of the first steps in this process is identifying eligible deposits. Not all deposits are treated equally. Lenders will exclude transfers between accounts, one-time windfalls, loans, or any non-business-related funds. What they want to see is true business revenue—money earned from providing goods or services. This is why clean and well-documented bank statements are so critical. If your deposits clearly reflect business activity, the underwriting process becomes much smoother and more favorable.

Once total eligible deposits are calculated, the next step is determining how much of that revenue can be used as qualifying income. This is where expense ratios come into play. Since business revenue is not the same as profit, lenders apply an expense factor to account for operating costs. For example, if a lender uses a 50% expense ratio, they assume that half of your revenue goes toward expenses, leaving the remaining 50% as usable income. This approach simplifies the underwriting process while still providing a reasonable estimate of your actual earnings.

However, not all borrowers are subject to the same expense ratio. This is where strategy becomes critical. If you can provide a CPA-prepared profit and loss statement that demonstrates lower expenses, you may be able to use a more favorable ratio, such as 30% or 40%. This can significantly increase your qualifying income and improve your loan eligibility. The key is ensuring that your P&L aligns with your bank statements and accurately reflects your business operations. Any discrepancies can create delays or even jeopardize your approval.

Another important factor lenders consider is the consistency of your income over time. They are not just looking at your highest months—they are averaging your income across the entire 12- or 24-month period. This means that fluctuations in revenue can impact your overall qualifying income. For example, if your business has strong seasonal performance but slower months during the year, those lower months will bring down your average. Understanding this helps you plan ahead and potentially choose the most favorable timeframe for your loan application.

Lenders also evaluate trends within your bank statements. An upward trend in revenue is generally viewed as positive, indicating growth and stability. A downward trend, however, may raise concerns about the sustainability of your income. If your most recent months show declining revenue, lenders may use a lower average or request additional documentation to verify that your business remains stable. This is why timing your application can be just as important as preparing your documentation.

In addition to income analysis, lenders assess the overall strength of your business. They may consider factors such as how long your business has been operating, the industry you are in, and the nature of your revenue streams. Businesses with longer operating histories and consistent income patterns are generally viewed as lower risk. Newer businesses may still qualify, but they often require stronger compensating factors, such as higher credit scores, larger down payments, or additional reserves.

The structure of your business also plays a role in how your income is evaluated. Sole proprietors may have simpler documentation requirements, while corporations and partnerships may require additional verification to confirm ownership and control of income. Regardless of structure, the goal is to clearly demonstrate that the deposits in your business account belong to you and can be used to support your mortgage payment. One of the most overlooked aspects of business bank statement loans is the importance of maintaining clean financial records. Mixing personal and business expenses can create confusion and reduce the amount of income that can be used for qualification. For example, if your business account includes large personal withdrawals or inconsistent spending patterns, lenders may apply a higher expense ratio or exclude certain deposits altogether. By keeping your accounts organized and separate, you create a clearer and more favorable financial profile.

Another key concept to understand is how lenders calculate your final qualifying income. After applying the expense ratio to your total deposits, they divide the remaining amount by the number of months reviewed to determine your average monthly income. This figure is then used to calculate your debt-to-income ratio and determine how much you can borrow. The higher your qualifying income, the greater your purchasing power.

It is also important to recognize that different lenders have different guidelines. Some may be more flexible with expense ratios, while others may have stricter requirements for documentation and consistency. This is why working with a knowledgeable mortgage professional who understands these programs can make a significant difference. Choosing the right lender can be just as important as preparing the right documentation. As you move forward in this book, you will begin to see that business bank statement lending is not just about meeting minimum requirements—it is about optimizing your financial profile. By understanding how lenders evaluate your income, you can make strategic decisions that improve your chances of approval and increase your borrowing capacity. This includes structuring your deposits, managing your expenses, and presenting your financial information in a way that aligns with underwriting guidelines.

Ultimately, the goal of this chapter is to give you a clear and practical understanding of how business bank statement income works. Once you understand the rules, you can begin to use them to your advantage. You can move from being reactive—hoping your loan gets approved—to being proactive—engineering your approval with confidence and precision. This is the foundation for everything that follows in this book.

Real-Life Math Example: Calculating Qualifying Income Using Business Bank Statements

To fully understand how business bank statement loans work, it is important to walk through a detailed real-life example that shows exactly how lenders calculate qualifying income. Imagine a borrower named Carlos who owns a small marketing agency. Carlos has been in business for four years and generates steady revenue through client contracts, digital campaigns, and consulting services. Like many business owners, Carlos takes advantage of tax deductions to reduce his taxable income, which makes it difficult for him to qualify using traditional loan programs. However, his business bank statements tell a different story—one of strong and consistent cash flow.

Carlos applies for a mortgage using 12 months of business bank statements. Over the past year, his total deposits are as follows: January $22,000, February $24,000, March $26,000, April $25,000, May $27,000, June $28,000, July $30,000, August $29,000, September $31,000, October $32,000, November $34,000, and December $36,000. When these deposits are added together, the total annual revenue reflected in his bank statements is $344,000.

The first step in the lender's analysis is to verify that these deposits are eligible. They review the statements and confirm that the majority of deposits come from business activity—client payments and service fees. A few transfers between accounts are identified and excluded, reducing the eligible deposit total slightly to $330,000. This adjusted figure represents the true business revenue that can be used for qualification.

Next, the lender applies an expense ratio. In Carlos's case, the lender offers two options. Without a CPA-prepared profit and loss statement, they apply a standard expense ratio of 50%. This means they assume that half of Carlos's revenue goes toward business expenses. Using this method, the lender calculates his qualifying income as $165,000 annually, which equals $13,750 per month.

However, Carlos works with his CPA to prepare a detailed profit and loss statement that shows his actual expenses are closer to 35% of revenue. This allows the lender to use a more favorable expense ratio. Instead of subtracting 50%, they now subtract 35%, leaving 65% of his revenue as qualifying income. Applying this ratio to the $330,000 in eligible deposits results in $214,500 of annual qualifying income, or $17,875 per month.

This difference is significant. By using a CPA-prepared P&L, Carlos increases his qualifying income by $4,125 per month. This directly impacts how much home he can afford. If the lender allows a debt-to-income ratio of 50%, Carlos could qualify for monthly housing payments of approximately $8,937 instead of $6,875. This could translate into hundreds of thousands of dollars in additional purchasing power.

The lender then averages Carlos's income over the 12-month

period. Even though his income increased throughout the year, they use the full average to ensure consistency. They also note the upward trend in his revenue, which strengthens his application and demonstrates business growth. This positive trend may also give the lender additional confidence in approving the loan.

Finally, the lender evaluates Carlos's overall financial profile, including his credit score, assets, and reserves. Because his business income is strong and well-documented, and his financial profile is stable, he is approved for the loan. The key takeaway from this example is that understanding how income is calculated allows borrowers to take control of the process.

This example highlights the power of business bank statement loans and the importance of strategy. By organizing his financials, working with a CPA, and choosing the right loan program, Carlos was able to qualify for a mortgage that would have been impossible using traditional methods. This is the opportunity available to you as well. When you understand how to turn your business revenue into qualifying income, you unlock a new level of financial flexibility and control.

Chapter 2

Revenue vs. Profit — How Lenders Convert Business Deposits into Qualifying Income

One of the most important concepts to fully understand when using business bank statements to qualify for a mortgage is the distinction between revenue and profit. This single concept determines how much income you can use, how large of a loan you can qualify for, and ultimately whether your file gets approved or not. Many borrowers assume that if their business generates significant deposits, they should automatically qualify for a large mortgage. However, lenders do not use gross revenue as income. Instead, they apply structured methods to estimate what portion of that revenue is actually usable after accounting for expenses. This chapter will break down that process in detail so you can understand exactly how your income is calculated and how to strategically improve it.

Revenue refers to the total amount of money your business generates before any expenses are deducted. This is the number reflected in your bank statement deposits. It includes payments from clients, customers, contracts, and services. Profit, on the other hand, is what remains after expenses such as payroll, marketing, rent, supplies, and other operating costs are deducted. Traditional mortgage lending relies heavily on profit as reported on tax returns, which is often reduced due to deductions. Business bank statement loans, however, start with revenue and then estimate profit using expense ratios or documented financial statements.

This distinction is critical because lenders are trying to determine your true ability to repay the loan. They understand that businesses have expenses, and they must account for those expenses when calculating qualifying income. The challenge is that they cannot rely solely on tax returns, so they use standardized methods to estimate net income. This is where expense ratios become the foundation of the calculation.

An expense ratio is the percentage of your revenue that is assumed to be spent on operating costs. For example, if a lender applies a 50% expense ratio, they assume that half of your revenue is used for expenses and the remaining half is your usable income. This means that if your business generates $300,000 in deposits, only $150,000 would be considered qualifying income under that assumption. While this may seem conservative, it provides a standardized way for lenders to evaluate different types of businesses without requiring detailed expense documentation in every case.

However, not all borrowers are limited to a fixed expense ratio. This is where strategy becomes essential. If you can demonstrate that your business operates with lower expenses, you may be able to qualify using a reduced expense ratio. This is typically done through a CPA-prepared profit and loss statement. When a licensed CPA verifies your business expenses and shows that they are lower than the lender's default assumption, the lender may use that lower percentage to calculate your income. This can significantly increase your qualifying income and improve your loan options.

Understanding how to position your business for a lower expense ratio is one of the most powerful tools you have. For example, service-based businesses often have lower overhead compared to product-based businesses. A consultant, coach, or digital service provider may operate with minimal expenses, allowing for a higher percentage of revenue to be counted as income. On the other hand, businesses that rely heavily on inventory, materials, or large teams may have higher expenses, which can reduce qualifying income. Knowing how your industry is perceived by lenders allows you to choose the right strategy and lender for your situation.

Another important factor is consistency. Lenders are not just looking at your total revenue—they are analyzing how stable and predictable your income is over time. If your business shows consistent deposits month after month, lenders are more confident in applying favorable assumptions. However, if your revenue fluctuates significantly, they may take a more conservative approach. This is why maintaining steady income patterns and avoiding large unexplained variations is so important.

The role of CPA-prepared profit and loss statements cannot be overstated. These documents provide a detailed breakdown of your revenue and expenses, giving lenders a clearer picture of your business operations. However, they must be accurate and consistent with your bank statements. If your P&L shows lower expenses but your bank statements suggest otherwise, it can create red flags and delay the approval process. The key is alignment—your documentation must tell a consistent story.

It is also important to understand that lenders may cap how low an expense ratio can go. Even if your CPA shows very low expenses, some lenders have minimum thresholds they will not go below. For example, a lender may not allow an expense ratio lower than 20% regardless of documentation. This is done to manage risk and ensure that income calculations remain realistic. Knowing these guidelines in advance helps you set realistic expectations and choose the right program.

Another concept to consider is how multiple business accounts are handled. If you operate multiple businesses or have multiple accounts, lenders may combine deposits to calculate total revenue. However, each account must be clearly documented and tied to your business activities. Mixing unrelated accounts or failing to properly document ownership can complicate the process and reduce qualifying income. Organization and clarity are key.

As you begin to understand these concepts, you will see that qualifying income is not just a number—it is the result of a structured process. By controlling the inputs into that process, you can influence the outcome. This includes how you manage your expenses, how you document your income, and how you present your financial profile. Small changes in these areas can lead to significant differences in your qualifying income.

Another powerful strategy is timing your application. If your business has recently improved profitability or reduced expenses, waiting until those changes are reflected in your bank statements and P&L can result in a higher qualifying income. Conversely, applying during a period of high expenses or inconsistent revenue can limit your options. Timing allows you to present your business in its strongest position.

It is also important to recognize that lenders are not just calculating income—they are assessing risk. A borrower with higher net income, consistent deposits, and well-documented financials is viewed as lower risk and more likely to be approved. By understanding how revenue is converted into profit and how profit is used for qualification, you can position yourself as a stronger borrower.

Ultimately, this chapter is about giving you control. Instead of being confused by how lenders calculate income, you now understand the mechanics behind it. You know how revenue is analyzed, how expense ratios are applied, and how documentation can influence the outcome. This knowledge allows you to move forward with confidence and make strategic decisions that improve your financial position.

Real-Life Math Example: Revenue vs. Profit and Expense Ratio Strategy

Let's walk through a detailed real-life example to show how revenue is converted into qualifying income and how different expense ratios can dramatically impact loan eligibility. Imagine a borrower named Sophia who owns an e-commerce business selling fitness equipment online. Her business has grown rapidly over the past two years, generating strong revenue but also incurring significant expenses related to inventory, shipping, and marketing.

Sophia applies for a mortgage using 24 months of business bank statements. Over this period, her total deposits equal $600,000, averaging $25,000 per month. At first glance, this appears to be a strong income profile. However, the lender must determine how much of this revenue can actually be used as qualifying income.

The lender begins by verifying eligible deposits. After excluding transfers and non-business-related deposits, the total eligible revenue is adjusted to $580,000. This becomes the basis for income calculation. Without additional documentation, the lender applies a standard expense ratio of 50%. This means they assume that half of Sophia's revenue goes toward expenses.

Using this assumption, the lender calculates Sophia's annual qualifying income as $290,000, or approximately $24,166 per month. While this is still a strong income, it may not fully reflect the efficiency of her business. Sophia knows that her actual expenses are closer to 40% of revenue, so she works with her CPA to prepare a detailed profit and loss statement.

The CPA-prepared P&L shows that Sophia's total expenses over the 24-month period were $232,000, leaving $348,000 in net income. This represents an expense ratio of 40% and a profit margin of 60%. Because this documentation is consistent with her bank statements, the lender agrees to use the lower expense ratio. With the updated ratio, Sophia's qualifying income increases significantly. Instead of using $290,000, the lender now uses $348,000 as her annual income, which equals $29,000 per month. This is an increase of nearly $5,000 per month compared to the original calculation.

This difference has a major impact on her loan eligibility. If the lender allows a 45% debt-to-income ratio, Sophia could qualify for monthly housing payments of approximately $13,050 instead of $10,875. This expanded capacity allows her to consider higher-priced properties or maintain greater financial flexibility.

Now consider a scenario where Sophia improves her business efficiency even further. By optimizing her supply chain and reducing marketing costs, she lowers her expense ratio to 35%. If this improvement is documented and reflected in her financials, her qualifying income would increase again.

Using a 35% expense ratio, her net income would be $377,000 annually, or approximately $31,416 per month. This would further increase her borrowing power and provide even more options in the housing market. This demonstrates how small improvements in expense management can lead to significant gains in qualifying income.

However, it is important to note that lenders will carefully review these figures for consistency. If Sophia's bank statements do not support the reduced expense ratio, the lender may revert to a higher assumption. This is why accurate documentation and alignment between financial records are essential.

This example illustrates the power of understanding revenue versus profit and how expense ratios shape your loan eligibility. By managing your business strategically, documenting your financials properly, and working with experienced professionals, you can significantly increase your qualifying income and achieve your real estate goals.

The key takeaway is that your income is not fixed—it is flexible within the structure of lending guidelines. By understanding how those guidelines work, you can position yourself for maximum success and take full advantage of the opportunities available through business bank statement mortgage loans.

Chapter 3

Using CPA-Prepared Profit & Loss Statements to Maximize Qualifying Income

As you continue building your mastery of business bank statement mortgage loans, one of the most powerful tools available to you is the CPA-prepared profit and loss statement. While bank statements provide the raw data of your business revenue, a properly structured profit and loss statement allows you to refine that data, justify lower expense ratios, and ultimately increase your qualifying income. This chapter is dedicated to helping you understand how to strategically use a CPA-prepared P&L to strengthen your mortgage application and unlock significantly greater borrowing power.

At its core, a profit and loss statement is a financial document that summarizes your business revenue, expenses, and net income over a specific period of time. Unlike tax returns, which are often optimized to minimize taxable income, a P&L used for mortgage qualification is designed to accurately reflect the operational reality of your business. This distinction is critical. When prepared correctly and supported by your bank statements, a CPA-prepared P&L can provide lenders with a more precise picture of your profitability, allowing them to move away from conservative assumptions and toward a more customized income calculation.

Without a CPA-prepared P&L, lenders typically rely on standardized expense ratios—often around 50%—to estimate your net income. While this simplifies the process, it may not accurately reflect your business. Many service-based businesses, digital businesses, consultants, and professionals operate with far lower expenses. If your true expense ratio is 30% or even 25%, using a default 50% assumption significantly understates your income and limits your loan potential. This is where the P&L becomes a game-changing tool.

A CPA-prepared P&L allows you to present your business in a structured, credible, and lender-friendly format. It shows exactly how much revenue your business generates and how much of that revenue is retained after expenses. More importantly, it provides third-party validation from a licensed professional, which gives lenders confidence in the accuracy of the numbers. This validation is often the difference between being stuck with a high expense ratio and qualifying with a much lower one.

However, not all P&Ls are created equal. For a P&L to be effective in the mortgage process, it must align with your bank statements. This means that the revenue reported on your P&L should closely match the deposits shown in your business accounts. If there is a significant discrepancy, lenders will question the accuracy of the document and may default back to a higher expense ratio or request additional documentation. Consistency is everything. Your financial story must be clear, logical, and verifiable.

Another critical aspect of the P&L is how expenses are categorized and presented. Lenders are not just looking at total expenses—they are evaluating the nature of those expenses. Some expenses may be considered necessary for business operations, while others may be viewed as discretionary or adjustable. By working with a knowledgeable CPA, you can ensure that your expenses are presented in a way that accurately reflects your business while also supporting your loan application. This does not mean manipulating numbers; it means organizing and documenting your financials in a clear and strategic manner.

Timing also plays a key role in using a CPA-prepared P&L. If your business has recently improved profitability, reduced expenses, or increased efficiency, capturing that improvement in a current P&L can significantly enhance your qualifying income. On the other hand, if your business experienced higher expenses in the past, waiting until your financials stabilize may result in a stronger application. The P&L allows you to present a more current and relevant picture of your business compared to historical tax returns.

It is also important to understand that lenders may have specific requirements for P&Ls. Some require year-to-date statements, while others may request trailing 12-month reports. In many cases, they will ask for both the P&L and supporting bank statements to ensure accuracy. Being prepared with these documents in advance can streamline the approval process and demonstrate professionalism and organization.

Another advantage of using a CPA-prepared P&L is the ability to explain your business. Numbers alone do not tell the full story. A well-prepared P&L, combined with a clear understanding of your business model, allows you to provide context for your income. For example, if your business has seasonal fluctuations, a P&L can show how those fluctuations balance out over time. If you have recently scaled your operations, it can demonstrate growth and increased profitability. This context helps lenders see beyond the raw numbers and understand the strength of your business.

The relationship between your P&L and your expense ratio is where the real power lies. By reducing your expense ratio, you increase the percentage of your revenue that can be used as qualifying income. This directly impacts your borrowing capacity. A small reduction in your expense ratio can translate into thousands of dollars in additional monthly income, which can significantly increase the size of the loan you qualify for. This is why mastering this concept is essential.

It is also worth noting that different lenders have different levels of flexibility when it comes to accepting CPA-prepared P&Ls. Some lenders are more aggressive and willing to use lower expense ratios if properly documented, while others may have minimum thresholds. Understanding these differences allows you to choose the right lender for your situation. This is not just about submitting documents—it is about matching your financial profile with the right program.

Another common question is whether you can prepare your own P&L. While self-prepared P&Ls may be accepted in some cases, they generally carry less weight than those prepared by a CPA. Lenders place a higher level of trust in documents that have been reviewed and signed by a licensed professional. If your goal is to maximize your qualifying income and strengthen your application, working with a CPA is often the best approach.

As you develop your strategy, you will begin to see that the P&L is not just a document—it is a tool for positioning. It allows you to present your business in the best possible light while remaining accurate and compliant. It bridges the gap between raw revenue and usable income, giving you control over how your financial profile is interpreted by lenders.

Ultimately, this chapter is about empowerment. By understanding how to use a CPA-prepared profit and loss statement, you gain the ability to influence one of the most important factors in your mortgage application—your qualifying income. Instead of being limited by default assumptions, you can take a proactive approach and create a financial profile that reflects your true earning potential.

Real-Life Math Example: How a CPA-Prepared P&L Increases Qualifying Income

Let's walk through a detailed example to illustrate how a CPA-prepared profit and loss statement can dramatically impact your qualifying income. Imagine a borrower named Daniel who owns a digital marketing agency. His business generates consistent revenue through monthly client retainers, project-based work, and online advertising services.

Daniel applies for a mortgage using 12 months of business bank statements. His total deposits over the past year are

$420,000, averaging $35,000 per month. After reviewing the statements, the lender identifies $400,000 as eligible business revenue after excluding transfers and non-business deposits. Without a CPA-prepared P&L, the lender applies a standard 50% expense ratio. This results in $200,000 of annual qualifying income, or approximately $16,666 per month. While this is a solid income, Daniel knows that his actual expenses are much lower because his business operates primarily online with minimal overhead.

Daniel works with his CPA to prepare a detailed profit and loss statement. The P&L shows that his total expenses for the year are $120,000, which represents an expense ratio of 30%. This means that 70% of his revenue is retained as profit. The CPA verifies these figures and ensures they align with Daniel's bank statements.

With this documentation, the lender agrees to use the lower expense ratio. Instead of using $200,000 as his qualifying income, they now use $280,000. This increases his monthly qualifying income to approximately $23,333. This is a difference of nearly $6,700 per month compared to the original calculation.

This increase has a major impact on Daniel's loan eligibility. If the lender allows a 50% debt-to-income ratio, Daniel could now qualify for monthly housing payments of approximately $11,666 instead of $8,333. This expanded capacity allows him to consider higher-value properties or maintain a stronger financial cushion. Now let's take the example one step further. Suppose Daniel continues to optimize his business and reduces his expenses to 25% of revenue. If this improvement is documented and supported by his financial records, his qualifying income would increase again. Using a 25% expense ratio, his net income would be $300,000 annually, or $25,000 per month.

At this level, Daniel's borrowing power increases even further. With a 50% debt-to-income ratio, he could qualify for monthly housing payments of $12,500. Compared to the original scenario using a 50% expense ratio, this represents a $4,167 increase in monthly capacity. Over the life of a loan, this can translate into hundreds of thousands of dollars in additional purchasing power.

However, it is important to remember that lenders will carefully review the P&L for accuracy and consistency. If the reported expenses do not align with the bank statements, the lender may question the validity of the document and revert to a higher expense ratio. This is why working with an experienced CPA and maintaining clean financial records is essential.

This example clearly demonstrates how a CPA-prepared profit and loss statement can transform your mortgage application. By accurately reflecting your business profitability and reducing your expense ratio, you can significantly increase your qualifying income and unlock greater opportunities in real estate.

The key takeaway is that your income is not fixed—it can be optimized through proper documentation and strategic planning. By leveraging a CPA-prepared P&L, you gain control over how your income is calculated and position yourself for maximum success in the mortgage approval process.

Chapter 4

Expense Ratio Strategies — How to Engineer Higher Qualifying Income

As you continue advancing through business bank statement mortgage loan strategies, you now arrive at one of the most powerful levers available to you: expense ratios. If revenue is the starting point and profit is the outcome, then the expense ratio is the mechanism that determines how much of your income is actually usable for mortgage qualification. Mastering expense ratio strategies is what separates average borrowers from highly strategic borrowers who are able to significantly increase their loan eligibility without increasing their revenue.

An expense ratio represents the percentage of your business revenue that is assumed to go toward operating expenses. In the context of business bank statement loans, lenders apply this ratio to your total eligible deposits to estimate your net income. The lower your expense ratio, the higher your qualifying income. This means that even if your revenue remains the same, adjusting your expense ratio can dramatically increase your borrowing power.

Most lenders begin with a standard expense ratio, often around 50%. This serves as a baseline assumption that half of your revenue is used for expenses. While this may be a reasonable estimate for many businesses, it is often overly conservative for others—especially service-based or digital businesses with low overhead. This is where strategy becomes critical. Your goal is to move away from generic assumptions and toward a customized expense ratio that accurately reflects your business.

The first step in optimizing your expense ratio is understanding your business model. Different industries have different cost structures. For example, a construction company or retail business may have higher expenses due to materials, labor, and inventory. On the other hand, a consultant, freelancer, or online business may have minimal expenses, allowing for a much lower expense ratio. Knowing where your business falls on this spectrum helps you determine what is realistic and achievable.

Once you understand your business model, the next step is documentation. Lenders will not simply accept a lower expense ratio without supporting evidence. This is where a CPA-prepared profit and loss statement becomes essential. As discussed in the previous chapter, a well-prepared P&L can validate your actual expenses and justify a lower ratio. However, it must be consistent with your bank statements and clearly reflect your business operations. Another important strategy is controlling how your expenses appear in your financial records. While you should never misrepresent your finances, you can make intentional decisions about how you manage and document expenses. For example, separating personal and business expenses ensures that your business accounts reflect only true operating costs. This creates a cleaner financial profile and prevents unnecessary increases in your expense ratio.

Timing also plays a significant role in expense ratio strategy. If your business has recently reduced expenses or improved efficiency, waiting until those changes are reflected in your financial statements can result in a more favorable ratio. Conversely, applying during a period of high expenses may limit your qualifying income. Strategic timing allows you to present your business in its strongest position.

Another advanced strategy involves understanding lender overlays. Not all lenders apply expense ratios in the same way. Some may allow ratios as low as 20% or 25% with proper documentation, while others may have minimum thresholds. By working with the right lender, you can take advantage of more flexible guidelines that align with your business. This is why choosing the right loan program is just as important as preparing the right documentation.

It is also important to understand how lenders interpret certain types of expenses. Some expenses may be considered fixed and necessary, while others may be viewed as variable or discretionary. For example, marketing expenses can often fluctuate and may be reduced if needed, while rent or payroll may be more consistent. By clearly documenting your expenses and demonstrating control over them, you can strengthen your case for a lower expense ratio.

Another key factor is consistency. Lenders want to see that your expense ratio is stable over time. If your expenses fluctuate significantly from month to month, it may raise concerns and lead to a more conservative approach. Maintaining consistent expense patterns helps build confidence and supports the use of a lower ratio.

As you refine your strategy, you will begin to see that expense ratio optimization is not just about reducing expenses—it is about presenting your business in a way that aligns with lender expectations. This includes organizing your financial records, maintaining clean accounts, and working with professionals who understand how to structure your documentation.

One of the most powerful aspects of expense ratio strategy is its direct impact on your qualifying income. Unlike increasing revenue, which may take time and effort, optimizing your expense ratio can produce immediate results. A reduction from 50% to 40% or even 30% can increase your qualifying income by thousands of dollars per month. This can significantly expand your loan options and allow you to pursue higher-value properties.

It is also important to recognize that expense ratio strategy is not a one-time effort. As your business evolves, your expenses may change. Continuously monitoring and optimizing your expense structure allows you to maintain a strong financial profile and take advantage of future opportunities. This is especially important if you plan to use business bank statement loans multiple times as part of a long-term real estate strategy.

Another advanced concept is combining expense ratio strategies with other income sources. For example, if you also have rental income or other streams of revenue, optimizing your business income can enhance your overall financial profile. This creates additional flexibility and increases your ability to qualify for larger loans or multiple properties.

Ultimately, this chapter is about giving you control over one of the most important variables in the mortgage qualification process. By understanding how expense ratios work and how to strategically influence them, you can transform your financial profile and unlock new opportunities. You are no longer limited by default assumptions—you are actively shaping the outcome.

Real-Life Math Example: How Expense Ratio Strategies Increase Borrowing Power

Let's walk through a detailed example to demonstrate how expense ratio strategies can dramatically impact qualifying income and loan eligibility. Imagine a borrower named Michael who owns a consulting business specializing in business development and sales training. His business generates consistent revenue through client contracts and workshops, with relatively low operating expenses.

Michael applies for a mortgage using 12 months of business bank statements. His total deposits for the year are $360,000, averaging $30,000 per month. After reviewing the statements, the lender identifies $340,000 as eligible business revenue after excluding transfers and non-business deposits.

In the initial scenario, Michael does not provide a CPA-prepared P&L, so the lender applies a standard 50% expense ratio. This results in $170,000 of annual qualifying income, or approximately $14,166 per month. Based on a 45% debt-to-income ratio, Michael could qualify for monthly housing payments of approximately $6,375.

However, Michael knows that his business operates with much lower expenses. He works with his CPA to prepare a detailed profit and loss statement that shows his actual expenses are only 35% of revenue. This means that 65% of his revenue is retained as profit.

With this documentation, the lender agrees to use the lower expense ratio. Applying a 35% expense ratio to the $340,000 in eligible deposits results in $221,000 of annual qualifying income, or approximately $18,416 per month. This is an increase of over $4,000 per month compared to the original calculation.

With this higher income, Michael's borrowing capacity increases significantly. At a 45% debt-to-income ratio, he can now qualify for monthly housing payments of approximately $8,287. This represents an increase of nearly $2,000 per month in housing capacity, which can translate into a much larger loan amount.

Now let's take the example further. Suppose Michael continues to optimize his business and reduces his expenses to 25% of revenue. If this improvement is documented and supported by his financial records, his qualifying income increases again. Using a 25% expense ratio, his net income would be $255,000 annually, or approximately $21,250 per month.

At this level, Michael's borrowing power expands even more. With a 45% debt-to-income ratio, he could qualify for monthly housing payments of approximately $9,562. Compared to the original scenario using a 50% expense ratio, this represents an increase of over $3,000 per month.

To put this into perspective, this increase in monthly capacity could allow Michael to qualify for a property that is hundreds of thousands of dollars more expensive, depending on interest rates and loan terms. This demonstrates how powerful expense ratio strategies can be in shaping your financial opportunities.

However, it is important to remember that lenders will carefully review all documentation. The CPA-prepared P&L must align with the bank statements, and the expense ratio must be reasonable for the type of business. Any inconsistencies can result in the lender reverting to a higher ratio or requesting additional documentation.

This example highlights the importance of understanding and applying expense ratio strategies. By taking control of how your income is calculated, you can significantly increase your qualifying income and expand your real estate opportunities. The key is to approach the process strategically, with a clear understanding of how lenders evaluate your financial profile and how you can position yourself for success.

Chapter 5

Structuring Your Business Bank Statements for Maximum Approval

As you continue building your expertise in business bank statement mortgage loans, you now arrive at one of the most practical and actionable areas of the entire process: how to structure your business bank statements for maximum approval. At this stage, you already understand how lenders calculate income, how expense ratios impact your qualifying income, and how CPA-prepared profit and loss statements can strengthen your application. Now, it is time to focus on the foundation of it all—the bank statements themselves.

Your bank statements are not just records of transactions; they are the primary story lenders use to evaluate your income, consistency, and business stability. Every deposit, every pattern, and every fluctuation contributes to how your financial profile is interpreted. The way your accounts are structured can either make your file clean, strong, and easy to approve—or confusing, inconsistent, and difficult to justify. This chapter will show you how to take control of that narrative.

The first and most important principle is separation. Your business and personal finances must be clearly separated. Mixing personal expenses with business deposits is one of the most common mistakes borrowers make, and it can significantly reduce your qualifying income. When personal transactions are mixed into business accounts, lenders may struggle to identify true business revenue, leading to excluded deposits or higher assumed expense ratios. By maintaining a dedicated business account for all business activity, you create a clean and transparent financial record that supports your application.

The second principle is consistency. Lenders are not just looking at total deposits—they are analyzing patterns over time. Consistent deposits that align with your business model signal stability and reliability. For example, if you receive regular payments from clients or customers on a predictable schedule, this strengthens your profile. On the other hand, irregular deposits, large unexplained spikes, or inconsistent income patterns can raise questions and lead to more conservative underwriting decisions.

Another critical factor is clarity. Your bank statements should clearly reflect the nature of your business activity. Deposits should be easily identifiable as business income. If your statements are filled with transfers between accounts, cash deposits without clear sources, or unrelated transactions, it becomes more difficult for lenders to determine what qualifies as income. Clear labeling, consistent deposit descriptions, and organized accounts all contribute to a stronger and more understandable financial profile.

Timing also plays an important role in structuring your bank statements. Because lenders typically review the most recent 12 or 24 months, the way your income appears during that period directly impacts your qualification. If your business has experienced growth, it is beneficial to ensure that your most recent months reflect that upward trend. If there have been periods of inconsistency or higher expenses, allowing time for stabilization before applying can improve your overall average income.

Another key strategy is managing large deposits. While large deposits can increase your total revenue, they can also raise questions if they are not consistent with your usual business activity. Lenders may ask for explanations or documentation to verify that these deposits are legitimate business income. If they cannot be verified, they may be excluded from your income calculation. This is why it is important to maintain documentation for significant transactions and ensure that your deposits align with your business model.

Expense management within your bank statements is equally important. While lenders primarily focus on deposits, they also review withdrawals to understand your expense patterns. If your account shows excessive or inconsistent spending, it may lead to higher assumed expense ratios. By maintaining a structured and predictable expense pattern, you can support a lower expense ratio and increase your qualifying income.

Another powerful strategy is minimizing unnecessary transfers between accounts. Frequent transfers can create confusion and make it difficult for lenders to distinguish between actual revenue and internal movement of funds. When possible, keep your revenue flowing directly into a primary business account and limit unnecessary movement. This simplifies the analysis and strengthens your file.

You should also be mindful of how you handle cash deposits. Cash deposits can be more difficult for lenders to verify, especially if they are not supported by clear documentation. While cash-based businesses can still qualify, maintaining detailed records and ensuring consistency is essential. Whenever possible, using traceable payment methods such as electronic transfers or checks can make your income easier to verify.

Another advanced strategy is aligning your bank statements with your P&L and overall financial narrative. All of your documentation should tell the same story. Your bank statements, P&L, and any additional documentation should be consistent and reinforce each other. When everything aligns, your file becomes stronger and easier to approve.

It is also important to understand that lenders are looking for risk indicators. Overdrafts, negative balances, or irregular account activity can raise concerns about financial management. Maintaining a positive balance, avoiding overdrafts, and demonstrating responsible account management all contribute to a stronger profile.

As you refine your approach, you will begin to see that structuring your bank statements is not just about organization—it is about strategy. You are intentionally creating a financial profile that aligns with lender expectations. You are removing confusion, highlighting strengths, and minimizing potential concerns. This proactive approach gives you control over how your income is interpreted.

Another key benefit of proper structuring is speed. Clean and organized bank statements lead to faster underwriting and fewer conditions. When lenders can easily understand your income, they are more likely to move your file forward quickly. This can make a significant difference in competitive markets where timing is critical. Ultimately, this chapter is about taking ownership of your financial presentation. Your bank statements are the foundation of your mortgage application, and how you manage them directly impacts your success. By applying the principles of separation, consistency, clarity, and strategy, you can transform your bank statements into a powerful tool for approval.

Real-Life Math Example: How Structuring Bank Statements Impacts Qualifying Income

Let's walk through a detailed example to show how the structure of your bank statements can directly impact your qualifying income and loan eligibility. Imagine a borrower named Alex who owns a home renovation business. His business generates strong revenue, but his bank statements are initially disorganized, with mixed personal and business transactions.

Over a 12-month period, Alex's total deposits equal $300,000. However, after reviewing his statements, the lender identifies several issues. Approximately $40,000 of the deposits are transfers between accounts, and another $20,000 consists of irregular deposits that cannot be clearly verified as business income. As a result, only $240,000 is considered eligible revenue.

Without a CPA-prepared P&L, the lender applies a 50% expense ratio. This results in $120,000 of annual qualifying income, or $10,000 per month. Based on a 45% debt-to-income ratio, Alex can qualify for monthly housing payments of approximately $4,500.

Now let's consider how restructuring his bank statements changes the outcome. Alex works with a mortgage professional and a CPA to reorganize his finances. He separates his personal and business accounts, eliminates unnecessary transfers, and ensures that all business deposits are clearly documented and consistent.

Over the next 12 months, Alex generates the same $300,000 in total deposits. However, because his accounts are now clean and organized, the lender is able to identify $285,000 as eligible business revenue. This is an increase of $45,000 in usable income compared to the previous scenario.

Alex also provides a CPA-prepared P&L showing that his actual expenses are 40% of revenue. With this documentation, the lender applies a 40% expense ratio instead of 50%. This results in $171,000 of annual qualifying income, or $14,250 per month.

This is a significant improvement from the original $10,000 per month. With the higher income, Alex's borrowing capacity increases substantially. At a 45% debt-to-income ratio, he can now qualify for monthly housing payments of approximately $6,412. This is an increase of nearly $2,000 per month compared to the original scenario. Now let's take the example even further. Suppose Alex continues to refine his financial structure and reduces his expense ratio to 30% through improved efficiency and documentation. Using this ratio, his qualifying income increases to $199,500 annually, or approximately $16,625 per month.

At this level, Alex's borrowing power expands even more. With a 45% debt-to-income ratio, he could qualify for monthly housing payments of approximately $7,481. Compared to the original scenario, this represents an increase of nearly $3,000 per month.

This example clearly demonstrates how structuring your bank statements can have a direct and powerful impact on your qualifying income. By organizing your accounts, reducing confusion, and aligning your documentation, you can significantly increase your loan eligibility without increasing your revenue.

The key takeaway is that your bank statements are not just a reflection of your business—they are a tool that can be optimized. By taking a strategic approach, you can transform your financial profile and position yourself for maximum success in the mortgage approval process.

Chapter 6

Advanced Income Analysis – Combining Business Bank Statements with Other Qualifying Strategies

As you progress deeper into mastering business bank statement mortgage loans, you begin to move beyond basic qualification and into advanced income structuring. At this level, you are no longer relying on a single source of income—you are strategically combining multiple income streams to maximize your borrowing power. This is where sophisticated borrowers gain a major advantage. By understanding how lenders allow different types of income to work together, you can significantly expand your loan eligibility and create opportunities that would not be possible using a single approach.

The foundation of advanced income analysis begins with recognizing that your business bank statement income is only one piece of your overall financial profile. Many borrowers also have additional income sources such as rental income, investment income, side businesses, or even part-time employment. When structured correctly, these income streams can be combined to create a stronger and more diversified profile. Lenders view diversified income as a positive factor because it reduces risk and demonstrates multiple sources of repayment.

One of the most common and powerful combinations is business bank statement income paired with rental income. For example, if you own investment properties that generate monthly cash flow, that income can often be added to your qualifying income. In some cases, lenders will use a percentage of the rental income—such as 75%—to account for vacancies and expenses. When combined with your business income, this can significantly increase your total qualifying income and allow you to qualify for larger loans or additional properties.

Another powerful strategy is combining business bank statement income with DSCR (Debt Service Coverage Ratio) loan strategies. While DSCR loans focus on the income generated by the property itself rather than the borrower's personal income, using both approaches together allows you to scale more effectively. You can use your business income to qualify for one property while using DSCR loans for others, creating a balanced and scalable portfolio strategy. This approach is particularly useful for real estate investors who want to grow quickly without being limited by traditional income requirements. In addition to rental income, some borrowers may have investment income from dividends, interest, or other sources. While these income streams are typically smaller, they can still contribute to your overall profile. Lenders may require documentation to verify the stability and continuity of this income, but when properly documented, it can provide an additional boost to your qualifying income.

Another advanced concept is the use of multiple businesses. If you operate more than one business, lenders may allow you to combine income from all of them, provided that each business is properly documented and stable. This can be particularly beneficial for entrepreneurs who have diversified their income across different ventures. However, each business must be evaluated individually, and the documentation must clearly demonstrate ownership and income flow.

It is also important to understand how lenders treat part-time or secondary employment. In some cases, if you have a history of consistent secondary income, it may be included in your qualification. This can provide additional flexibility, especially if your business income fluctuates. The key is demonstrating consistency and reliability over time.

Another critical aspect of advanced income analysis is understanding how lenders calculate your total qualifying income. Each income source is evaluated separately and then combined to create a total monthly income figure. This figure is then used to calculate your debt-to-income ratio. The higher your total qualifying income, the more flexibility you have in terms of loan size and payment capacity.

However, combining income sources also requires careful documentation. Each source must be clearly verified and supported by appropriate documentation. This includes bank statements, lease agreements, tax returns, or other relevant records. The goal is to create a cohesive financial profile that clearly demonstrates your ability to repay the loan.

Another advanced strategy is layering income to offset weaknesses in one area. For example, if your business income has some variability, adding stable rental income can help balance your profile. Similarly, if your rental income is limited, strong business income can compensate. This layered approach allows you to present a more stable and reliable financial picture.

It is also important to consider reserves and liquidity. Lenders often require borrowers to have a certain amount of reserves—funds available after closing—to ensure that they can continue making payments. Having multiple income streams can help you build these reserves more easily and strengthen your overall application.

As you move into more advanced strategies, you will begin to see that mortgage qualification is not just about meeting requirements—it is about building a comprehensive financial profile. You are combining income sources, optimizing documentation, and strategically positioning yourself for approval. This approach allows you to operate at a higher level and take advantage of opportunities that others may not even be aware of.

Another key concept is scalability. By combining income sources, you are not just qualifying for one loan—you are creating a system that can be used repeatedly. This is particularly important for investors who want to build a portfolio over time. By understanding how to structure your income, you can continue to qualify for additional properties and expand your investments.

Ultimately, this chapter is about expanding your perspective. Instead of thinking about income as a single number, you begin to see it as a combination of multiple streams that can be structured and optimized. This mindset allows you to move beyond limitations and create a financial profile that supports your long-term goals.

Real-Life Math Example: Combining Multiple Income Streams for Maximum Qualification

Let's walk through a detailed example to illustrate how combining multiple income streams can significantly increase your qualifying income and borrowing power. Imagine a borrower named Lisa who owns a consulting business and also has rental properties that generate monthly income.

Lisa applies for a mortgage using 12 months of business bank statements. Her total eligible business deposits are $360,000 for the year, which equals $30,000 per month. After applying a 40% expense ratio based on a CPA-prepared P&L, her qualifying business income is $216,000 annually, or $18,000 per month.

On its own, this is a strong income. However, Lisa also owns two rental properties. Each property generates $2,500 per month in rental income, for a total of $5,000 per month. Lenders typically use 75% of rental income to account for expenses and vacancies, so Lisa's qualifying rental income is $3,750 per month.

When combined, Lisa's total qualifying income becomes $21,750 per month. This is a significant increase compared to her business income alone. Using a 45% debt-to-income ratio,

Lisa can now qualify for monthly housing payments of approximately $9,787.

Now let's take the example further. Lisa also has a small investment portfolio that generates $1,000 per month in dividend income. With proper documentation, the lender includes this income in her profile. This increases her total qualifying income to $22,750 per month.

At this level, her borrowing capacity increases even further. With a 45% debt-to-income ratio, she can now qualify for monthly housing payments of approximately $10,237. This additional income provides more flexibility and allows her to consider higher-value properties.

Now consider a more advanced scenario. Lisa decides to purchase an additional investment property using a DSCR loan. This property generates $3,000 per month in rental income and qualifies based on its own cash flow. While this income may not be fully counted in her personal income, it strengthens her overall financial profile and allows her to continue scaling her portfolio.

By combining business income, rental income, and investment income, Lisa creates a diversified and powerful financial profile. Each income stream contributes to her overall qualification, allowing her to maximize her borrowing power and achieve her real estate goals.

This example demonstrates the importance of thinking strategically about income. Instead of relying on a single source, you can combine multiple streams to create a stronger and more flexible profile. This approach not only increases your loan eligibility but also provides greater financial stability and long-term growth potential.

The key takeaway is that your income is not limited to one source—it is a combination of all the resources available to you. By understanding how to structure and combine these income streams, you can unlock new opportunities and take your mortgage strategy to the next level.

Chapter 7

Red Flags, Underwriting Risks, and How to Strengthen Your File

As you move into the more advanced stages of mastering business bank statement mortgage loans, it becomes critical to understand not just what helps you get approved—but what can hurt your chances. Many borrowers focus only on income and overlook the subtle red flags that underwriters look for when reviewing a file. These red flags can reduce qualifying income, trigger additional conditions, delay approvals, or even lead to outright denials. The goal of this chapter is to help you think like an underwriter, identify potential risks in your financial profile, and proactively strengthen your file before it is ever submitted.

Underwriting is fundamentally about risk assessment. Lenders are not just verifying income—they are evaluating the likelihood that you will continue to earn that income and successfully repay the loan. Every aspect of your bank statements, financial behavior, and documentation contributes to that assessment. When your file is clean, consistent, and well-structured, it signals stability and reliability. When inconsistencies or irregularities appear, they raise questions that must be resolved before approval can be granted. One of the most common red flags in business bank statement loans is inconsistent deposits. Lenders expect to see a pattern of regular income that aligns with your business model. If your deposits fluctuate significantly from month to month without a clear explanation, it can create uncertainty about your income stability. For example, a business that shows $40,000 in one month and $10,000 in the next may raise concerns unless there is a clear and documented reason, such as seasonality or contract-based payments. Consistency builds confidence, while volatility introduces risk.

Another major red flag is declining income. Lenders pay close attention to trends, particularly in the most recent months. Even if your overall average income is strong, a downward trend can signal potential instability. For example, if your income has steadily decreased over the last three to six months, the lender may question whether that trend will continue. In some cases, they may use a lower income calculation based on recent months or require additional documentation to justify the decline. Understanding this allows you to time your application strategically and present your business during a period of stability or growth.

Large unexplained deposits are another area of concern. While large deposits can increase your total revenue, they can also raise questions if they do not fit your normal business pattern.

Lenders will want to verify that these deposits are legitimate business income and not loans, gifts, or one-time events. If you cannot provide clear documentation, these deposits may be excluded from your income calculation, reducing your qualifying income. Maintaining records and ensuring that your deposits align with your business activity is essential.

Excessive transfers between accounts can also complicate the underwriting process. When funds are moved frequently between accounts, it becomes difficult for lenders to distinguish between actual revenue and internal transfers. This can lead to confusion, additional documentation requests, and potential exclusion of certain deposits. Minimizing unnecessary transfers and keeping your income flow straightforward helps create a clearer financial picture.

Another important red flag is overdrafts or negative balances. These indicate potential cash flow management issues and can raise concerns about your ability to handle financial obligations. Even if your overall income is strong, frequent overdrafts may lead lenders to view your file as higher risk. Maintaining a positive balance and demonstrating responsible account management is critical.

Mixing personal and business finances is another common issue that can weaken your file. When personal expenses are paid from business accounts or vice versa, it creates confusion and makes it harder for lenders to identify true business income. This can lead to higher assumed expense ratios or exclusion of certain deposits. Keeping your accounts separate and clearly organized is one of the simplest yet most effective ways to strengthen your application.

Irregular expense patterns can also impact how your income is perceived. If your expenses vary significantly without explanation, lenders may apply a more conservative expense ratio. For example, if your account shows large spikes in spending during certain months, it may suggest higher operating costs than initially assumed. Consistency in your expense patterns supports a lower expense ratio and strengthens your overall profile.

Another factor lenders consider is the nature of your business. Some industries are viewed as more stable than others. For example, professional services, healthcare, and established trades may be seen as lower risk compared to newer or highly volatile industries. While you cannot change your industry, you can strengthen your file by demonstrating consistency, growth, and strong financial management within your field.

Documentation gaps are another potential red flag. Missing bank statements, incomplete records, or inconsistencies between documents can delay the process and raise concerns. Lenders rely on complete and accurate documentation to make decisions. Being organized and prepared with all required documents helps streamline the process and build confidence.

One of the most effective ways to strengthen your file is to anticipate these red flags and address them proactively. This means reviewing your bank statements before applying, identifying any potential issues, and taking steps to resolve them. For example, if you have irregular deposits, you can prepare explanations and supporting documentation. If your income has fluctuated, you can provide context and demonstrate stability over time.

Another powerful strategy is working with experienced professionals who understand these loan programs. A knowledgeable mortgage broker or loan officer can help you identify potential issues and guide you in structuring your file for maximum approval. This collaboration can make a significant difference in the outcome of your application.

It is also important to understand that not all red flags are deal-breakers. Many issues can be explained and mitigated with proper documentation and context. The key is transparency and consistency. When your financial story is clear and supported by documentation, lenders are more likely to work with you and find solutions. As you continue to refine your approach, you will begin to see that strengthening your file is not about perfection—it is about preparation. By understanding how underwriters think and what they look for, you can position yourself as a strong and reliable borrower. This proactive approach gives you control over the process and increases your chances of approval.

Ultimately, this chapter is about shifting your perspective. Instead of reacting to underwriting conditions, you are anticipating them. Instead of hoping your file is strong enough, you are intentionally building a file that meets and exceeds lender expectations. This level of preparation is what separates successful borrowers from those who struggle with the process.

Real-Life Math Example: How Red Flags Impact Qualifying Income and Approval

Let's walk through a detailed example to illustrate how red flags can affect your qualifying income and how addressing them can significantly improve your outcome. Imagine a borrower named David who owns a landscaping business. His business generates strong revenue, but his bank statements contain several issues that initially weaken his application.

Over a 12-month period, David's total deposits equal $280,000. At first glance, this appears to be a solid income profile. However, upon closer review, the lender identifies several red flags. Approximately $30,000 of the deposits are large, irregular transactions that do not match his typical business activity. Another $20,000 consists of transfers between accounts. After excluding these amounts, the lender determines that only $230,000 qualifies as eligible revenue.

Additionally, David's bank statements show inconsistent monthly deposits. Some months reflect $30,000 in revenue, while others drop to $12,000. This variability raises concerns about income stability. As a result, the lender takes a more conservative approach and applies a 55% expense ratio instead of the standard 50%.

Using these assumptions, David's qualifying income is calculated at $103,500 annually, or approximately $8,625 per month. Based on a 45% debt-to-income ratio, he can qualify for monthly housing payments of approximately $3,881. This limits his borrowing power and reduces his options.

Now let's see how addressing these red flags changes the outcome. David works with a mortgage professional to review his financials and make improvements. He provides documentation for the large deposits, showing that they are legitimate business income from larger projects. This allows the lender to include an additional $25,000 in revenue, increasing his eligible deposits to $255,000. David also stabilizes his income by restructuring his billing process, creating more consistent monthly deposits. Over time, his bank statements reflect a more predictable income pattern. This reduces concerns about volatility and allows the lender to apply a lower expense ratio of 45%.

With these improvements, David's qualifying income increases significantly. Using a 45% expense ratio on $255,000 in revenue results in $140,250 annually, or approximately $11,687 per month. This is an increase of over $3,000 per month compared to the original calculation.

At this higher income level, David's borrowing capacity expands. With a 45% debt-to-income ratio, he can now qualify for monthly housing payments of approximately $5,259. This is an increase of nearly $1,400 per month, which can translate into a substantially larger loan amount.

Now let's take the example one step further. David continues to improve his financial profile by separating his personal and business accounts, eliminating unnecessary transfers, and maintaining consistent deposits. He also works with a CPA to document his expenses more accurately, reducing his expense ratio to 40%.

With this final optimization, his qualifying income increases to $153,000 annually, or $12,750 per month. At a 45% debt-to-income ratio, he can now qualify for monthly housing payments of approximately $5,737. Compared to the original scenario, this represents an increase of nearly $2,000 per month.

This example clearly demonstrates how red flags can impact your qualifying income and how addressing them can dramatically improve your outcome. By identifying and resolving issues, providing documentation, and structuring your financials strategically, you can transform your file from a high-risk profile into a strong and competitive application.

The key takeaway is that underwriting is not just about numbers—it is about perception. When your financial profile is clear, consistent, and well-documented, lenders see you as a lower-risk borrower and are more willing to approve your loan. By understanding and managing red flags, you take control of that perception and position yourself for success.

Chapter 8

Choosing the Right Lender and Program — How to Match Your File to the Best Approval Strategy

At this stage in your journey through business bank statement mortgage loan mastery, you have developed a deep understanding of how income is calculated, how expense ratios influence qualifying income, how to structure your bank statements, and how to avoid red flags. Now comes one of the most critical decisions in the entire process—choosing the right lender and loan program. This decision can determine not only whether you get approved, but also how much you qualify for, what terms you receive, and how smooth the process will be.

Many borrowers assume that all lenders operate under the same guidelines, but this is far from the truth. In reality, business bank statement loan programs can vary significantly from one lender to another. These differences include how income is calculated, what expense ratios are allowed, how strictly documentation is reviewed, and what compensating factors are required. Understanding these variations allows you to strategically match your financial profile to the lender that offers the most favorable outcome. The first concept to understand is that lenders operate within guidelines, but they also have overlays. Overlays are additional requirements or restrictions that go beyond standard program guidelines. For example, one lender may allow a minimum expense ratio of 25% with a CPA-prepared P&L, while another may require at least 40% regardless of documentation. These differences can dramatically impact your qualifying income and borrowing power. Choosing the right lender means finding one whose overlays align with your strengths.

Another key factor is how lenders evaluate risk. Some lenders are more conservative and prioritize stability and consistency, while others are more flexible and willing to work with unique financial profiles. If your income is highly consistent and your documentation is clean, a conservative lender may offer competitive terms. However, if your income is more complex or includes variability, a more flexible lender may be better suited to your situation.

Loan program structure is another important consideration. Some lenders offer 12-month bank statement programs, while others require 24 months. A 12-month program may be beneficial if your recent income is strong and shows an upward trend. On the other hand, a 24-month program may provide a more stable average if your income has fluctuated.

Understanding which timeframe works best for your situation allows you to present your strongest financial profile.

Interest rates and loan terms also vary between lenders. While business bank statement loans typically have slightly higher rates than traditional loans, the difference between lenders can still be significant. Some lenders may offer more competitive rates but have stricter guidelines, while others may offer more flexibility at a higher cost. Balancing these factors is essential to finding the right program.

Another important factor is loan-to-value (LTV) limits. Different lenders have different maximum LTV ratios, which determine how much you can borrow relative to the property value. Some lenders may allow higher LTVs for strong borrowers, while others may require larger down payments. Understanding these limits helps you plan your investment and choose a program that aligns with your financial goals.

Reserve requirements are another key consideration. Lenders often require borrowers to have a certain amount of reserves—funds available after closing—to ensure they can continue making payments. These requirements can vary based on the loan amount, property type, and borrower profile. Having sufficient reserves not only meets lender requirements but also strengthens your application and may lead to better terms. Another advanced concept is compensating factors. These are strengths in your financial profile that can offset potential weaknesses. For example, a high credit score, significant reserves, or a strong income trend can compensate for minor inconsistencies in your bank statements. Different lenders weigh these factors differently, so choosing a lender that values your strengths can improve your chances of approval.

Working with the right mortgage professional is also critical. An experienced broker or loan officer who understands business bank statement programs can help you navigate the options and identify the best fit for your situation. They can also help you package your file in a way that highlights your strengths and aligns with lender expectations. This guidance can make a significant difference in both approval and efficiency.

Another important strategy is pre-qualification. Before committing to a lender, it is beneficial to review your financial profile and determine which programs you are most likely to qualify for. This allows you to approach the process with confidence and avoid unnecessary denials or delays. Pre-qualification also helps you set realistic expectations for loan terms and affordability.

It is also important to consider long-term strategy. The lender you choose for your current loan may not be the same lender you use for future transactions. As your financial profile evolves, you may qualify for different programs or better terms. Understanding this allows you to view each loan as part of a broader strategy rather than a one-time event.

Another key factor is communication and responsiveness. The mortgage process involves multiple steps and requires coordination between various parties. Working with a lender who communicates clearly and responds promptly can make the process smoother and less stressful. This is especially important in competitive markets where timing can impact your ability to secure a property.

As you refine your approach, you will begin to see that choosing the right lender is not just about finding a loan—it is about aligning your financial profile with the right opportunity. It is about understanding your strengths, identifying the programs that best match those strengths, and positioning yourself for success.

Ultimately, this chapter is about strategy and alignment. You have already done the work of building a strong financial profile. Now, you must ensure that profile is presented to the right lender under the right program. When these elements align, approvals become smoother, terms become more favorable, and opportunities expand.

Real-Life Math Example: How Choosing the Right Lender Changes Your Loan Outcome

Let's walk through a detailed example to illustrate how choosing the right lender and program can significantly impact your qualifying income and loan eligibility. Imagine a borrower named Sarah who owns a consulting business. Her business generates consistent revenue, and she is applying for a mortgage using business bank statements.

Over a 12-month period, Sarah's total eligible deposits are $360,000, averaging $30,000 per month. She provides a CPA-prepared P&L showing that her actual expenses are 35% of revenue, resulting in a qualifying income of $234,000 annually, or $19,500 per month.

Now let's compare how two different lenders evaluate her file.

Lender A is more conservative and has stricter overlays. They require a minimum expense ratio of 45% regardless of the P&L. Using this ratio, Sarah's qualifying income is reduced to $198,000 annually, or $16,500 per month. At a 45% debt-to-income ratio, she can qualify for monthly housing payments of approximately $7,425.

Lender B is more flexible and allows the use of her CPA-prepared P&L with a 35% expense ratio. Using this ratio, her qualifying income remains $234,000 annually, or $19,500 per month. At the same 45% debt-to-income ratio, she can qualify for monthly housing payments of approximately $8,775.

This difference of $1,350 per month in qualifying capacity can translate into a significantly larger loan amount. Depending on interest rates and loan terms, this could mean the ability to purchase a property that is hundreds of thousands of dollars more expensive.

Now let's take the example further. Lender A also requires 24 months of bank statements, which includes a period where Sarah's income was lower. This reduces her average monthly income to $15,000, further limiting her borrowing capacity. Lender B, on the other hand, allows a 12-month program that reflects her current, higher income.

With the 12-month program, Sarah's qualifying income remains strong, and her borrowing capacity increases. This demonstrates how program structure can impact your outcome just as much as expense ratios.

Additionally, Lender B offers a slightly higher interest rate but allows a higher loan-to-value ratio, reducing the amount of cash Sarah needs to bring to closing. This provides greater flexibility and allows her to preserve capital for other investments. By choosing Lender B, Sarah is able to maximize her qualifying income, increase her borrowing power, and maintain greater financial flexibility. This example highlights the importance of aligning your financial profile with the right lender and program.

The key takeaway is that not all lenders are the same. The way your income is calculated, the guidelines applied, and the overall structure of the loan can vary significantly. By understanding these differences and choosing the right lender, you can dramatically improve your loan outcome and achieve your real estate goals more effectively.

Chapter 9

Overcoming Credit Challenges and Weak Profiles with Business Bank Statement Loans

As you continue progressing through the Bank Statement Mortgage Loan Mastery Series, you now arrive at one of the most impactful and empowering topics in modern lending: how to get approved even when your credit profile is not perfect. Many borrowers assume that strong credit is the only path to mortgage approval, but business bank statement loans offer a different perspective. These programs are designed to evaluate the full financial picture—not just a credit score—and that opens the door for borrowers who may have experienced challenges in the past but have rebuilt their income and financial stability.

The reality is that credit issues are common. Life happens. People experience job transitions, business downturns, unexpected expenses, or economic shifts that can impact their credit profile. Late payments, high utilization, collections, or even major credit events such as bankruptcies or foreclosures can appear on a credit report. Traditional loan programs often treat these issues as disqualifying factors, but alternative documentation loans—like business bank statement programs—take a more flexible and holistic approach.

The first step in overcoming credit challenges is understanding how lenders view risk. Credit score is one component of that risk, but it is not the only one. Lenders also evaluate income, reserves, business stability, and overall financial behavior. A borrower with strong, consistent business income and significant reserves may still be considered a strong candidate even with a lower credit score. This is where the power of business bank statement loans becomes clear—they allow you to offset weaknesses in one area with strengths in another.

One of the most important concepts in this process is compensating factors. These are strengths in your financial profile that help balance out potential risks. For example, if your credit score is lower, you may still qualify by demonstrating strong and consistent income, maintaining substantial cash reserves, or providing a larger down payment. Lenders look at the total picture, and the more strengths you can present, the more confidence they have in approving your loan.

Another key factor is credit event seasoning. If you have experienced a major credit event such as a bankruptcy, foreclosure, or short sale, lenders will typically require a certain amount of time to pass before you can qualify. This is known as seasoning. The required timeframe varies depending on the lender and the type of event, but it is often shorter for non-QM programs compared to traditional loans. Understanding these timelines allows you to plan your application and apply when you are most likely to be approved.

It is also important to address any recent credit issues before applying. Lenders pay close attention to recent activity, and recent late payments or high utilization can raise concerns. By stabilizing your credit in the months leading up to your application, you can improve your profile and increase your chances of approval. This may include paying down balances, avoiding new debt, and ensuring that all accounts are current.

Another powerful strategy is managing your debt-to-income ratio. Even if your credit score is lower, a strong income combined with manageable debt can create a favorable profile. Business bank statement loans allow you to maximize your qualifying income, which can help offset higher debt levels. This is why understanding income calculation and expense ratios is so important—it directly impacts your ability to overcome credit challenges.

Reserves also play a critical role in strengthening your application. Lenders want to see that you have sufficient funds available after closing to cover your mortgage payments. This provides an additional layer of security and demonstrates financial stability. For borrowers with credit challenges, having strong reserves can significantly improve the likelihood of approval.

Another important consideration is loan structure. In some cases, adjusting the loan structure can improve your chances of approval. This may include increasing your down payment, choosing a lower loan amount, or selecting a program with more flexible guidelines. By working with an experienced mortgage professional, you can identify the structure that best aligns with your financial profile.

It is also important to understand that not all lenders treat credit challenges the same way. Some lenders are more flexible and specialize in working with borrowers who have non-traditional profiles. Choosing the right lender is critical, as it can determine whether your file is viewed as a risk or as an opportunity. This reinforces the importance of aligning your financial profile with the right program and lender.

Another key concept is documentation and explanation. If there are specific issues in your credit history, providing clear explanations and supporting documentation can help address lender concerns. For example, if a late payment was due to a temporary hardship that has since been resolved, explaining the situation can provide context and demonstrate that the issue is unlikely to recur.

As you continue to refine your approach, you will begin to see that overcoming credit challenges is not about hiding weaknesses—it is about addressing them and strengthening the overall profile. Transparency, consistency, and preparation are the keys to success. When lenders see a borrower who understands their financial situation and has taken steps to improve it, they are more likely to work toward approval.

Another important mindset shift is viewing credit as one part of a larger strategy. While improving your credit is always beneficial, it should not be the only focus. By building strong income, maintaining reserves, and structuring your financial profile effectively, you can create multiple pathways to approval. This diversified approach gives you more options and reduces your reliance on any single factor.

Ultimately, this chapter is about empowerment. Credit challenges do not have to define your financial future. With the right knowledge, strategy, and preparation, you can overcome these obstacles and achieve your real estate goals.

Business bank statement loans provide a pathway for borrowers who are financially strong but may not fit traditional lending criteria.

Real-Life Math Example: Overcoming Credit Challenges with Strong Income and Strategy

Let's walk through a detailed example to illustrate how a borrower can overcome credit challenges using business bank statement income and strategic planning. Imagine a borrower named Kevin who owns a construction business. Kevin has experienced strong business growth over the past two years, but his credit profile includes some challenges due to past financial difficulties.

Kevin's credit score is 640, which is lower than what is typically required for conventional loans. He also had a late payment history two years ago, but his recent credit activity has been stable. Despite these challenges, Kevin's business generates strong and consistent income.

Over a 12-month period, Kevin's business bank statements show total deposits of $400,000. After excluding transfers and non-business deposits, the lender determines that $380,000 is eligible revenue. Kevin provides a CPA-prepared P&L showing that his expenses are 45% of revenue, resulting in a qualifying income of $209,000 annually, or approximately $17,416 per month.

On its own, this is a strong income profile. However, Kevin's credit score presents a potential challenge. To strengthen his application, Kevin focuses on compensating factors. He has $100,000 in reserves, which demonstrates financial stability. He also plans to make a 25% down payment, reducing the lender's risk.

Using a 45% debt-to-income ratio, Kevin can qualify for monthly housing payments of approximately $7,837. This provides a solid foundation for his loan application. However, let's see how additional strategies can further improve his position.

Kevin works on improving his credit by paying down existing balances and ensuring all accounts remain current. Over a few months, his credit score increases to 680. While this may seem like a small improvement, it can have a meaningful impact on lender perception and loan terms.

Additionally, Kevin reduces his expense ratio by optimizing his business operations. With updated financials and documentation, his CPA prepares a new P&L showing expenses at 40% of revenue. This increases his qualifying income to $228,000 annually, or $19,000 per month.

With this higher income, Kevin's borrowing capacity increases. At a 45% debt-to-income ratio, he can now qualify for monthly housing payments of approximately $8,550. This is an increase of over $700 per month compared to the previous scenario.

Now let's consider the impact of choosing the right lender. Kevin works with a lender who specializes in business bank statement loans and is more flexible with credit profiles. This lender places greater emphasis on his strong income and reserves rather than focusing solely on his credit score.

With the combination of strong income, improved credit, significant reserves, and a larger down payment, Kevin is approved for the loan. This example demonstrates how multiple factors work together to overcome credit challenges.

The key takeaway is that credit is just one piece of the puzzle. By strengthening other areas of your financial profile, you can offset credit weaknesses and create a compelling case for approval. Business bank statement loans provide the flexibility needed to make this possible.

This example also highlights the importance of strategy. Kevin did not rely on a single solution—he improved his credit, optimized his income, increased his reserves, and chose the right lender. By combining these strategies, he was able to achieve his goal of homeownership despite initial challenges.

The lesson here is clear: your financial future is not limited by your past. With the right approach, you can overcome obstacles, strengthen your profile, and take control of your mortgage journey.

Chapter 10

Advanced Bank Statement Mortgage Loan Structuring — Engineering Approvals with Precision

As you reach the final chapter of this book, you are no longer approaching business bank statement mortgage loans as a borrower—you are approaching them as a strategist. You now understand income calculation, expense ratios, CPA-prepared documentation, lender selection, red flags, and how to overcome credit challenges. Chapter 10 brings all of these elements together into one powerful concept: engineering your approval.

Engineering an approval means taking full control of your financial profile and intentionally structuring every component of your loan application to align with lender guidelines. Instead of asking, "Will I qualify?" you begin asking, "How do I structure my file to ensure approval and maximize my outcome?" This shift in mindset is what separates advanced borrowers from the average applicant.

The first principle of advanced structuring is understanding that every variable in your loan file can be adjusted. Your income, expense ratio, documentation, reserves, credit positioning, and even the lender you choose all work together to determine your approval. By optimizing each of these variables, you can significantly improve your chances of success and increase your borrowing power.

One of the most powerful tools in advanced structuring is income layering. Rather than relying on a single income source, you combine multiple streams—business bank statement income, rental income, investment income, or even secondary employment—to create a stronger overall profile. This layered approach not only increases your qualifying income but also demonstrates diversification, which lenders view as a positive factor.

Another key strategy is timing your application. Your financial profile is constantly evolving, and applying at the right time can make a significant difference. For example, if your business has recently experienced growth, waiting until your bank statements reflect that increase can result in a higher qualifying income. Similarly, if you have recently improved your credit or reduced your expenses, allowing those changes to stabilize before applying can strengthen your file.

Expense ratio optimization remains a central component of advanced structuring. As you have learned, even small adjustments to your expense ratio can lead to substantial increases in qualifying income. By working with a CPA, organizing your financials, and choosing lenders with flexible guidelines, you can position yourself to use the lowest reasonable expense ratio for your business.

Another important factor is loan-to-value (LTV) strategy. The amount of your down payment directly impacts lender risk and can influence approval. A higher down payment reduces risk and may allow for more favorable terms or approval in cases where other factors are weaker. Conversely, maintaining a lower down payment may preserve liquidity but require stronger compensating factors. Understanding how to balance these trade-offs is a key part of advanced structuring.

Reserves and liquidity also play a critical role. Lenders want to see that you have the ability to continue making payments even if your income fluctuates. By maintaining strong reserves, you not only meet lender requirements but also strengthen your overall profile. In some cases, higher reserves can offset other weaknesses and improve your chances of approval.

Another advanced concept is file presentation. How your documentation is organized and presented can significantly impact how underwriters perceive your application. A clean, well-structured file with clear documentation, consistent numbers, and logical explanations creates confidence. On the other hand, a disorganized file with inconsistencies can lead to delays and additional conditions. Presentation is not just about aesthetics—it is about clarity and credibility.

Choosing the right lender remains a critical component of advanced structuring. As discussed in the previous chapter, different lenders have different guidelines and levels of flexibility. By matching your financial profile to the right lender, you can take advantage of favorable terms and increase your chances of approval. This is not a one-size-fits-all process—it requires careful analysis and strategic decision-making.

Another powerful strategy is scenario planning. Before submitting your application, you can evaluate different scenarios to determine the best approach. For example, you may compare the impact of using a 12-month versus a 24-month bank statement program, or analyze how different expense ratios affect your qualifying income. By exploring these options in advance, you can choose the strategy that produces the best outcome.

It is also important to consider long-term planning. Advanced structuring is not just about your current loan—it is about creating a system that allows you to continue qualifying for future opportunities. By maintaining strong financial habits, optimizing your income, and building reserves, you can position yourself for ongoing success in real estate and beyond.

Another key mindset shift is viewing your financial profile as dynamic rather than static. You have the ability to influence how your income is calculated, how your expenses are perceived, and how your overall profile is evaluated. This means you are not limited by your current situation—you can actively shape your outcome through strategy and preparation.

As you bring all of these elements together, you will begin to see that mortgage approval is not a mystery—it is a structured process that can be understood and optimized. By mastering the concepts in this book, you have gained the tools needed to navigate that process with confidence and precision.

Ultimately, this chapter is about empowerment and control. You are no longer reacting to lender requirements—you are anticipating them. You are not just submitting an application—you are engineering a solution. This level of understanding allows you to achieve your goals more efficiently and with greater certainty.

Real-Life Math Example: Engineering a Mortgage Approval for Maximum Borrowing Power

Let's walk through a comprehensive example that brings together all the strategies discussed in this book. Imagine a borrower named Rachel who owns a consulting business and is looking to purchase a high-value property. Rachel wants to maximize her borrowing power while maintaining financial flexibility.

Rachel's business generates $480,000 in total deposits over a 12-month period. After excluding ineligible deposits, the lender determines that $450,000 is eligible revenue. Rachel works with her CPA to prepare a profit and loss statement showing that her expenses are 35% of revenue.

Using this expense ratio, Rachel's qualifying income is calculated at $292,500 annually, or approximately $24,375 per month. On its own, this is a strong income profile. However, Rachel wants to increase her borrowing power even further.

Rachel also owns a rental property that generates $3,000 per month in income. After applying a 75% factor, her qualifying rental income is $2,250 per month. This increases her total qualifying income to $26,625 per month.

Using a 45% debt-to-income ratio, Rachel can now qualify for monthly housing payments of approximately $11,981. This provides a strong foundation, but Rachel explores additional strategies to further optimize her profile.

She decides to increase her down payment from 20% to 25%, reducing the lender's risk and improving her approval terms. She also ensures that she has six months of reserves after closing, which strengthens her application and provides additional security.

Rachel then evaluates different lender options. One lender requires a 40% expense ratio, while another allows her CPA-documented 35% ratio. By choosing the more flexible lender, she preserves her higher qualifying income.

Next, Rachel considers timing. Her business has shown growth over the past six months, so she chooses a 12-month program that reflects her higher recent income rather than a 24-month program that would include lower earlier months.

With all these strategies combined, Rachel's final qualifying income remains at $26,625 per month, but her overall profile is significantly stronger. The lender views her as a low-risk borrower due to her strong income, reserves, and structured application.

Now let's compare this to a less optimized scenario. If Rachel had used a 40% expense ratio, excluded rental income, and applied with a lower down payment, her qualifying income might have been closer to $22,000 per month. At a 45% debt-to-income ratio, this would limit her monthly housing capacity to $9,900. By applying advanced structuring strategies, Rachel increases her monthly capacity by over $2,000. This can translate into a significantly larger loan amount and greater purchasing power.

This example demonstrates how combining multiple strategies—expense ratio optimization, income layering, lender selection, timing, and reserves—can dramatically improve your outcome. Each decision contributes to the overall result, and when combined, they create a powerful and optimized financial profile.

The key takeaway from this final chapter is that mortgage approval is not a fixed outcome—it is a process that can be engineered. By understanding the variables and applying strategic thinking, you can take control of your financial future and achieve your real estate goals with confidence.

Chapter 11

Scaling with Business Bank Statement Loans — Building a Long-Term Real Estate and Financing Strategy

As you move beyond the fundamentals and advanced structuring of business bank statement mortgage loans, the next level is understanding how to use these tools repeatedly to scale your wealth, expand your portfolio, and build long-term financial stability. This chapter is not about qualifying for one loan—it is about creating a system that allows you to qualify again and again, using your business income as a foundation for growth.

At this stage, your mindset shifts from borrower to investor. Instead of asking, "Can I get approved?" you begin asking, "How can I structure my income and finances so I can continue getting approved for future opportunities?" This is where business bank statement loans become more than just a financing option—they become a strategic asset.

The first principle of scaling is sustainability. Your ability to qualify for future loans depends on maintaining consistent and well-documented income. This means continuing to manage your business in a way that supports stable deposits, clean bank statements, and optimized expense ratios. Every financial decision you make today impacts your ability to qualify tomorrow. By maintaining discipline in your financial structure, you create a foundation for ongoing success.

Another key concept is repeatability. The strategies you have learned in this book—structuring bank statements, optimizing expense ratios, using CPA-prepared P&Ls, and choosing the right lenders—can be applied repeatedly. Once you understand the system, you can replicate it for future transactions. This creates a cycle where each successful loan builds momentum for the next.

Portfolio growth is a central focus of scaling. Many borrowers begin with a primary residence or a single investment property, but the goal is to expand over time. By leveraging your business income, you can continue acquiring properties while maintaining control over your financing strategy. This is particularly powerful when combined with other loan types, such as DSCR loans, which allow properties to qualify based on their own income.

Another important aspect of scaling is cash flow management. As you acquire more properties or take on additional financial obligations, it becomes critical to ensure that your income supports your expenses. This includes not only your mortgage payments but also property maintenance, taxes, insurance, and other costs. By maintaining a strong cash flow position, you reduce risk and strengthen your ability to qualify for future loans.

Reserves play an increasingly important role as you scale. Lenders often require higher reserves for borrowers with multiple properties or larger loan amounts. Building and maintaining these reserves not only meets lender requirements but also provides a safety net that allows you to navigate fluctuations in income or market conditions. Strong reserves are a key indicator of financial stability and can significantly improve your approval profile.

Another advanced strategy is leveraging equity. As your properties appreciate in value, you can use that equity to access additional capital through refinancing or cash-out strategies. This allows you to reinvest in new opportunities without relying solely on your business income. Combining equity strategies with business bank statement loans creates a powerful system for growth.

Diversification is also essential in a long-term strategy. Relying on a single income source or property type can increase risk. By diversifying your income streams and investment portfolio, you create a more stable and resilient financial profile. This not only improves your ability to qualify for loans but also protects you against market fluctuations.

Another key factor is understanding lender limits and exposure. Some lenders have limits on the number of properties or total loan exposure they are willing to extend to a single borrower. As you scale, you may need to work with multiple lenders or diversify your financing sources. This requires planning and coordination to ensure that your growth strategy remains aligned with lender guidelines.

Timing remains an important consideration. As your portfolio grows, you will need to strategically plan when to apply for new loans. This includes ensuring that your income, credit, and reserves are in optimal condition at the time of application. Proper timing allows you to present your strongest financial profile and maximize your chances of approval.

Another critical aspect of scaling is documentation. As your financial profile becomes more complex, maintaining organized and accurate records becomes even more important. This includes bank statements, P&Ls, tax documents, and property records. Clear and consistent documentation supports your application and reduces the likelihood of delays or complications. Working with experienced professionals becomes increasingly valuable as you scale. A knowledgeable mortgage broker, CPA, and financial advisor can help you navigate complex situations, identify opportunities, and optimize your strategy. This collaborative approach allows you to operate at a higher level and make more informed decisions.

Another powerful concept is leverage. By using financing strategically, you can control larger assets with less capital. This allows you to expand your portfolio more quickly while preserving liquidity for future opportunities. However, leverage must be managed carefully to ensure that your cash flow remains positive and sustainable.

As you continue to grow, you will begin to see the compounding effect of your strategy. Each property, each loan, and each financial decision builds on the previous one. Over time, this creates a portfolio that generates income, builds equity, and supports your long-term goals.

Ultimately, this chapter is about vision and execution. You are no longer focused on a single transaction—you are building a system that supports ongoing growth. By applying the principles in this book and maintaining a disciplined approach, you can use business bank statement loans as a foundation for long-term success in real estate and beyond.

Real-Life Math Example: Scaling a Portfolio Using Business Bank Statement Loans

Let's walk through a detailed example to illustrate how a borrower can use business bank statement loans to scale a real estate portfolio over time. Imagine a borrower named Anthony who owns a successful consulting business and wants to build a portfolio of investment properties.

Anthony's business generates $500,000 in annual deposits. After excluding ineligible deposits, the lender determines that $470,000 is eligible revenue. Anthony provides a CPA-prepared P&L showing an expense ratio of 40%, resulting in a qualifying income of $282,000 annually, or $23,500 per month.

Using a 45% debt-to-income ratio, Anthony can qualify for monthly housing payments of approximately $10,575. He uses this capacity to purchase his first investment property, which has a monthly mortgage payment of $3,000 and generates $3,500 in rental income.

After accounting for a 75% rental income factor, the lender considers $2,625 as qualifying rental income. This additional income increases Anthony's total qualifying income to $26,125 per month. With this increased income, Anthony's borrowing capacity expands. He now has the ability to take on additional properties while maintaining a manageable debt-to-income ratio. Over time, he repeats this process, using his business income and rental income to qualify for new loans.

After acquiring three properties, each generating similar rental income, Anthony's total rental income becomes $10,500 per month, with $7,875 considered for qualification. Combined with his business income, his total qualifying income reaches $31,375 per month.

At this level, Anthony's borrowing capacity increases significantly. With a 45% debt-to-income ratio, he can qualify for monthly housing payments of approximately $14,118. This allows him to continue expanding his portfolio.

Anthony also builds equity in his properties as they appreciate in value. After a few years, he refinances one of his properties and accesses $100,000 in equity, which he uses as a down payment for another investment property. This accelerates his growth and allows him to scale more quickly.

By maintaining consistent business income, optimizing his expense ratio, and strategically combining income sources, Anthony creates a system that supports ongoing expansion. Each property contributes to his overall income and strengthens his financial profile. This example demonstrates how business bank statement loans can be used not just for a single purchase, but as part of a long-term strategy for building wealth. By understanding how to structure your income, manage your finances, and leverage opportunities, you can create a scalable system that supports your goals.

The key takeaway is that scaling is not about taking unnecessary risks—it is about applying proven strategies consistently over time. With the right approach, you can use your business income as a foundation for growth and create a portfolio that generates income, builds equity, and provides long-term financial security.

Chapter 12

Final Strategy, Execution Plan, and Long-Term Wealth Blueprint Using Business Bank Statement Loans

As you reach the final chapter of this book, everything you have learned now comes together into one unified system. This is where knowledge becomes execution and execution becomes results. You are no longer just learning how business bank statement mortgage loans work—you are now building a repeatable blueprint that can be used to create long-term wealth, financial flexibility, and control over your future.

This chapter is about turning strategy into action. It is about taking everything from income calculation, expense ratio optimization, CPA-prepared documentation, lender selection, red flag management, and scaling strategies—and combining them into a clear execution plan. The goal is to ensure that you are not just informed, but fully prepared to take the next step with confidence.

The first principle of your long-term blueprint is clarity. You must define your goals. Are you purchasing a primary residence? Are you building a rental portfolio? Are you focused on cash flow, appreciation, or a combination of both? Your strategy will vary depending on your objectives. Clarity allows you to align your financing approach with your long-term vision.

Once your goals are defined, the next step is building your financial foundation. This includes structuring your business income, maintaining clean and consistent bank statements, and optimizing your expense ratio. These elements form the core of your qualification strategy. Without a strong foundation, it becomes difficult to scale effectively.

Another critical component is documentation readiness. Before applying for any loan, you should have your bank statements, CPA-prepared P&L, and supporting documentation organized and aligned. This not only speeds up the approval process but also demonstrates professionalism and reliability to lenders. A well-prepared file creates confidence and reduces friction.

Timing is another key factor in execution. You should aim to apply when your financial profile is at its strongest. This means stable or increasing income, optimized expense ratios, improved credit, and sufficient reserves. Strategic timing allows you to present your best possible profile and maximize your approval potential.

Another important element is lender alignment. As you have learned, not all lenders are the same. Choosing the right lender and program is critical to achieving the best outcome. This requires understanding your strengths and matching them with lenders who value those strengths. The right alignment can significantly increase your qualifying income and improve your loan terms.

Your execution plan should also include a reserve strategy. Maintaining sufficient reserves is not just about meeting lender requirements—it is about creating financial security. Reserves provide a buffer that allows you to navigate unexpected expenses or income fluctuations. They also strengthen your application and increase lender confidence.

Another key component of your blueprint is leverage. By using financing strategically, you can control larger assets with less capital. This allows you to expand your portfolio more quickly and take advantage of opportunities as they arise. However, leverage must be used responsibly. Maintaining positive cash flow and managing risk are essential to long-term success.

As you begin to execute your plan, you will also need to focus on consistency. Success in this space is not achieved through a single transaction—it is built over time through repeated, disciplined actions. By maintaining consistent income, clean financial records, and strategic planning, you create a system that supports ongoing growth.

Another powerful concept is reinvestment. As you generate income and build equity, you can reinvest those resources into new opportunities. This creates a compounding effect where each success builds on the previous one. Over time, this can lead to significant growth in both income and net worth.

It is also important to continuously evaluate and refine your strategy. Markets change, lending guidelines evolve, and your personal goals may shift. By staying informed and adapting your approach, you can continue to optimize your results and take advantage of new opportunities.

Working with the right team is another essential element of your blueprint. A knowledgeable mortgage professional, CPA, and financial advisor can provide valuable guidance and help you navigate complex situations. This collaborative approach allows you to operate more efficiently and make better decisions.

Another key mindset is viewing your financial profile as an asset. Your income, documentation, and financial structure are tools that can be optimized and leveraged. By treating your financial profile as something you actively manage and improve, you gain greater control over your opportunities.

As you implement your strategy, you will begin to see the cumulative impact of your efforts. Each loan, each property, and each financial decision contributes to your overall growth. Over time, this creates a portfolio that generates income, builds equity, and supports your long-term goals.

Ultimately, this chapter is about execution and vision. You have the knowledge, the tools, and the strategies needed to succeed. Now it is about taking action, staying consistent, and building a system that works for you. Business bank statement loans are not just a financing option—they are a pathway to financial independence when used strategically.

Real-Life Math Example: Building a Long-Term Wealth Blueprint with Business Bank Statement Loans

Let's walk through a comprehensive example that demonstrates how a borrower can implement a long-term strategy using business bank statement loans. Imagine a borrower named Maria who owns a digital services business and wants to build a portfolio of income-producing properties.

Maria's business generates $600,000 in annual deposits. After excluding ineligible deposits, the lender determines that $560,000 is eligible revenue. Maria works with her CPA to prepare a profit and loss statement showing an expense ratio of 35%, resulting in a qualifying income of $364,000 annually, or approximately $30,333 per month. Using a 45% debt-to-income ratio, Maria can qualify for monthly housing payments of approximately $13,650. She uses this capacity to purchase her first property, which has a monthly mortgage payment of $4,000 and generates $4,500 in rental income.

After applying a 75% rental income factor, the lender considers $3,375 as qualifying rental income. This increases Maria's total qualifying income to $33,708 per month.

With this increased income, Maria's borrowing capacity expands. She uses this additional capacity to acquire a second property with similar financials. Now, her total rental income increases, further strengthening her profile.

After acquiring three properties, each generating $4,500 per month, Maria's total rental income reaches $13,500 per month, with $10,125 considered for qualification. Combined with her business income, her total qualifying income reaches $40,458 per month.

At this level, Maria's borrowing capacity increases significantly. With a 45% debt-to-income ratio, she can qualify for monthly housing payments of approximately $18,206. This allows her to continue expanding her portfolio and taking advantage of new opportunities.

Maria also builds equity in her properties as they appreciate in value. After a few years, she refinances one of her properties and accesses $150,000 in equity, which she uses as a down payment for another investment. This accelerates her growth and allows her to scale more quickly.

Additionally, Maria maintains strong reserves by setting aside a portion of her income. This not only meets lender requirements but also provides financial security and flexibility. Her strong reserves and consistent income make her an attractive borrower, allowing her to access better loan terms over time.

By consistently applying the strategies outlined in this book—optimizing income, managing expenses, choosing the right lenders, and reinvesting her gains—Maria creates a scalable and sustainable system for building wealth.

This example illustrates how business bank statement loans can be used as part of a long-term strategy. By combining income, leveraging opportunities, and maintaining discipline, Maria is able to build a portfolio that generates income, builds equity, and supports her financial goals.

The key takeaway is that success is not about a single transaction—it is about building a system. With the right approach, you can use business bank statement loans to create a long-term wealth blueprint that provides financial freedom and control over your future.

Chapter 13

Exit Strategies, Portfolio Optimization, and Long-Term Financial Control

As you continue advancing beyond acquisition and scaling, the next level of mastery is understanding how and when to exit, optimize, and reposition your portfolio. Many borrowers focus heavily on getting approved and acquiring properties, but true financial control comes from knowing how to manage, restructure, and eventually exit investments in a way that maximizes returns while minimizing risk. This chapter is about turning your portfolio into a dynamic system—one that you actively manage, refine, and optimize over time.

The first concept to understand is that every property you acquire should have an exit strategy from the very beginning. An exit strategy is your plan for how you will eventually extract value from the property. This could include selling the property for appreciation, refinancing to access equity, converting it to a different use, or holding it long-term for cash flow. Without a clear exit strategy, you risk becoming reactive rather than strategic.

One of the most common exit strategies is appreciation-based selling. As property values increase over time, you can sell the asset and capture the gain. This strategy is particularly effective in strong markets where property values are rising. However, timing is critical. Selling too early may limit your gains, while holding too long may expose you to market downturns. Understanding market cycles and monitoring property performance allows you to make informed decisions.

Another powerful strategy is refinancing. Instead of selling a property, you can refinance it to access the equity you have built. This allows you to pull out cash while retaining ownership of the asset. This cash can then be reinvested into new opportunities, creating a cycle of growth. Cash-out refinancing is one of the most effective ways to scale a portfolio without selling assets.

Portfolio optimization is another critical concept. As your portfolio grows, not all properties will perform equally. Some may generate strong cash flow, while others may underperform or require significant maintenance. Regularly evaluating your portfolio allows you to identify which assets are contributing to your goals and which may need to be repositioned or sold.

Cash flow analysis plays a central role in this process. Each property should be evaluated based on its income, expenses, and overall return. Properties with strong and consistent cash flow provide stability and support your ability to qualify for additional financing. Properties with weak cash flow may need to be improved, restructured, or replaced.

Another important factor is leverage management. While leverage allows you to control more assets with less capital, it also increases risk. As your portfolio grows, it is important to maintain a balance between growth and stability. This may involve paying down certain loans, refinancing to better terms, or adjusting your debt structure to reduce risk.

Tax strategy is also a key component of long-term financial control. Different exit strategies have different tax implications. For example, selling a property may trigger capital gains taxes, while refinancing does not. Understanding these implications allows you to plan your exits in a way that maximizes your net returns. Working with a knowledgeable CPA or tax advisor is essential in this area.

Another advanced concept is repositioning assets. This involves changing how a property is used or managed to increase its value or income potential. For example, converting a long-term rental into a short-term rental, improving the property to increase rent, or changing management strategies can all enhance performance. Repositioning allows you to extract more value from existing assets without acquiring new ones. Diversification continues to play an important role at this stage. As your portfolio grows, spreading your investments across different property types, locations, and income streams can reduce risk and increase stability. This diversified approach helps protect your portfolio from market fluctuations and creates multiple avenues for growth.

Another key aspect of optimization is liquidity management. While real estate is a powerful wealth-building tool, it is not always liquid. Ensuring that you have access to cash or liquid assets allows you to take advantage of opportunities and handle unexpected expenses. Balancing real estate investments with liquid reserves is essential for long-term success.

As you refine your strategy, you will begin to see that your portfolio is not static—it is constantly evolving. Each decision you make, whether it is acquiring, refinancing, or selling, shapes your overall financial position. By approaching your portfolio with a strategic mindset, you can continuously improve its performance and align it with your goals.

Another important mindset shift is viewing your portfolio as a business. Just as you manage your primary business with strategy and intention, your real estate portfolio should be managed with the same level of attention. This includes tracking performance, analyzing returns, and making data-driven decisions. Long-term financial control comes from understanding that you have multiple options at every stage. You can hold, sell, refinance, or reposition your assets depending on market conditions and your personal goals. This flexibility allows you to adapt and thrive in changing environments.

Ultimately, this chapter is about mastery. You are no longer just acquiring assets—you are actively managing and optimizing them. You are making strategic decisions that maximize returns, minimize risk, and support your long-term vision. This is where true financial independence begins to take shape.

Real-Life Math Example: Optimizing and Exiting a Portfolio for Maximum Returns

Let's walk through a detailed example to illustrate how exit strategies and portfolio optimization can impact your financial outcomes. Imagine a borrower named Daniel who has built a portfolio of four investment properties using business bank statement loans.

Each property was purchased for $300,000 with a 20% down payment, resulting in loan amounts of $240,000 per property. Over time, the properties have appreciated to $400,000 each.

This means Daniel now has $160,000 in equity per property, or a total of $640,000 across his portfolio. Each property generates $2,500 per month in rental income, for a total of $10,000 per month. After expenses and mortgage payments, Daniel nets approximately $1,000 per property, or $4,000 per month in cash flow.

Daniel now evaluates his options. One option is to sell one of the properties. If he sells a property for $400,000, after paying off the $240,000 loan, he is left with $160,000 before transaction costs and taxes. After accounting for these costs, he may net approximately $140,000.

Alternatively, Daniel considers a cash-out refinance. By refinancing a property at 75% loan-to-value, he can take out a new loan of $300,000. After paying off the existing $240,000 loan, he receives $60,000 in cash. This allows him to access equity without selling the property.

If Daniel refinances two properties, he can access $120,000 in cash, which he can use as down payments for additional investments. This allows him to expand his portfolio while maintaining ownership of his existing assets.

Now let's analyze the impact on his income. If Daniel uses the $120,000 to purchase another property that generates $2,500 per month in rent, he increases his total rental income to

$12,500 per month. This additional income strengthens his financial profile and increases his ability to qualify for future loans. Daniel also evaluates the performance of each property. One property is generating lower cash flow due to higher maintenance costs. He decides to sell this underperforming asset and reinvest the proceeds into a higher-performing property. This improves his overall portfolio performance and increases his net income.

By combining refinancing, selling, and reinvesting strategies, Daniel is able to optimize his portfolio. He increases his income, maintains strong equity positions, and continues to grow his investments.

This example demonstrates how strategic decision-making can significantly impact your financial outcomes. By understanding your options and applying the right strategies, you can maximize returns and maintain control over your portfolio.

The key takeaway is that your portfolio is not just a collection of properties—it is a system that can be optimized and refined over time. By actively managing your assets and making strategic decisions, you can create a powerful engine for long-term wealth and financial independence.

Chapter 14

Building a Legacy — Protecting, Transferring, and Expanding Wealth with Business Bank Statement Loan Strategies

As you reach this stage of your journey, your focus expands beyond acquisition, scaling, and optimization. You begin to think about legacy. Not just how to build wealth, but how to protect it, grow it across generations, and ensure that the system you have created continues to produce results long after your initial efforts. This chapter is about transforming your strategy into a long-term legacy plan—one that provides financial security, opportunity, and stability for you and those who follow.

The concept of legacy begins with protection. As your portfolio grows and your income increases, it becomes increasingly important to safeguard your assets. This includes structuring ownership in a way that reduces risk and protects against potential liabilities. Many investors use business entities such as LLCs to hold properties, creating a layer of separation between personal and business assets. This structure not only protects your wealth but also creates a more organized and scalable framework for growth.

Another critical aspect of protection is insurance. Adequate coverage ensures that your assets are protected against unforeseen events such as damage, liability claims, or loss of income. As your portfolio expands, reviewing and adjusting your insurance strategy becomes essential. This is not just about meeting minimum requirements—it is about ensuring that your investments are fully protected.

Estate planning is another key component of building a legacy. This involves creating a clear plan for how your assets will be transferred to the next generation. Without proper planning, your estate may be subject to delays, legal complications, or unnecessary taxes. By working with legal and financial professionals, you can create a structure that ensures a smooth and efficient transfer of wealth.

Trusts are often used as part of this strategy. They allow you to control how and when your assets are distributed, providing flexibility and protection. For example, you may choose to distribute income from your properties to beneficiaries while retaining control over the assets themselves. This creates a balance between providing financial support and maintaining long-term stability. Another important concept is continuity. Your business and real estate portfolio should be structured in a way that allows them to continue operating even if you are no longer actively involved. This may involve establishing management systems, hiring professionals, or creating clear operational guidelines. Continuity ensures that your assets continue to generate income and support your legacy.

Education is also a key component of legacy building. Providing the next generation with the knowledge and tools to manage and grow your assets is essential. This includes teaching financial literacy, investment principles, and the strategies you have used to build your portfolio. A well-informed successor is more likely to preserve and expand the wealth you have created.

Another powerful strategy is expansion. Legacy is not just about preserving what you have—it is about continuing to grow and evolve. This may involve exploring new markets, diversifying into different asset classes, or leveraging new financing strategies. By staying adaptable and forward-thinking, you can ensure that your legacy continues to expand over time.

Tax efficiency remains an important consideration. Structuring your investments and transactions in a way that minimizes tax liabilities allows you to retain more of your wealth and pass on greater value. This may include strategies such as 1031 exchanges, which allow you to defer capital gains taxes when reinvesting in new properties. Understanding and applying these strategies is essential for long-term wealth preservation.

Another key aspect of legacy building is maintaining strong financial habits. The discipline and consistency that allowed you to build your portfolio must continue as you manage and expand it. This includes monitoring cash flow, maintaining reserves, and making strategic decisions. These habits form the foundation of long-term success.

As you move forward, you will begin to see that your role evolves from builder to steward. You are no longer just creating wealth—you are managing and guiding it. This requires a different mindset, one that focuses on sustainability, responsibility, and long-term impact.

Another important concept is flexibility. Markets change, opportunities evolve, and new challenges arise. By maintaining a flexible approach and staying informed, you can adapt your strategy and continue to thrive in changing conditions. This adaptability is a key factor in building a lasting legacy.

Collaboration also becomes increasingly important. Working with a team of professionals—such as attorneys, CPAs, and financial advisors—allows you to make informed decisions and navigate complex situations. This team-based approach ensures that your strategy remains aligned with your goals.

Ultimately, building a legacy is about more than financial success. It is about creating a system that provides security, opportunity, and growth for future generations. It is about leaving behind something that continues to create value and impact long after your initial efforts.

Real-Life Math Example: Building and Transferring a Legacy Portfolio

Let's walk through a detailed example to illustrate how a borrower can build, protect, and transfer a legacy portfolio using business bank statement loan strategies. Imagine a borrower named Sophia who has built a portfolio of five investment properties over time.

Each property was purchased for $350,000 with a 20% down payment, resulting in loan amounts of $280,000 per property. Over several years, the properties have appreciated to $500,000 each. This means Sophia now has $220,000 in equity per property, or a total of $1,100,000 in equity across her portfolio.

Each property generates $3,000 per month in rental income, for a total of $15,000 per month. After expenses and mortgage payments, Sophia nets approximately $1,200 per property, or

$6,000 per month in cash flow. Sophia decides to structure her portfolio within an LLC to protect her assets and create a more organized framework. This allows her to separate her personal and business finances and reduce potential liability.

She also establishes a trust to manage the transfer of her assets to her children. The trust outlines how the properties will be managed and how income will be distributed. This ensures that her portfolio continues to generate income for her family while maintaining long-term stability.

Now let's analyze the financial impact. Sophia's portfolio generates $72,000 per year in net cash flow. Over time, this income can be reinvested into additional properties or used to support her family's financial needs.

Sophia also considers a 1031 exchange strategy. She sells one of her properties for $500,000 and reinvests the proceeds into a larger property valued at $800,000. By using a 1031 exchange, she defers capital gains taxes and increases her income potential.

The new property generates $5,000 per month in rental income, increasing her total rental income to $17,000 per month. This improves her cash flow and strengthens her overall portfolio.

Sophia also builds reserves by setting aside a portion of her income. Over time, she accumulates $200,000 in reserves, providing financial security and flexibility for future opportunities.

As Sophia's portfolio continues to grow, she involves her children in the management process, teaching them how to analyze properties, manage finances, and make strategic decisions. This ensures that her legacy continues beyond her direct involvement.

This example demonstrates how combining acquisition, protection, and strategic planning can create a powerful legacy. By structuring her assets, optimizing her portfolio, and preparing the next generation, Sophia is able to build a system that provides long-term value and stability.

The key takeaway is that legacy is not built by chance—it is created through intentional strategy and disciplined execution. By applying the principles in this book, you can build a portfolio that not only supports your financial goals but also creates lasting impact for generations to come.

Chapter 15

Mastery, Freedom, and the Final Blueprint — Turning Strategy into Lifelong Financial Control

You have now reached the final chapter of this book, and with it, the culmination of everything you have learned throughout this series. This is where knowledge transforms into mastery, and mastery transforms into freedom. Up to this point, you have built a deep understanding of business bank statement mortgage loans, income structuring, expense ratio optimization, lender alignment, scaling strategies, risk management, and long-term wealth building. Now, the final step is integrating all of these elements into a lifelong system—one that gives you complete control over your financial future.

This chapter is not about learning new concepts—it is about solidifying your mindset and refining your execution. It is about stepping into a position where you are no longer dependent on traditional systems, but instead operate with clarity, confidence, and control. Financial freedom is not just about income—it is about having options, flexibility, and the ability to make decisions on your own terms. The first principle of mastery is awareness. You now understand how lenders think, how income is evaluated, and how financial profiles are structured. This awareness gives you an advantage that most borrowers do not have. You are no longer navigating the process blindly—you are making informed decisions based on a clear understanding of the system.

The second principle is control. You have learned that your financial profile is not fixed—it can be shaped and optimized. You can influence your qualifying income through expense ratios, structure your bank statements for clarity, choose the right lender, and position your application strategically. This level of control allows you to approach financing with confidence rather than uncertainty.

Another key aspect of mastery is consistency. The strategies in this book are not one-time actions—they are habits. Maintaining clean financial records, optimizing your income, and making strategic decisions must become part of your routine. Consistency is what allows you to sustain and grow your success over time.

Freedom comes from the ability to make choices without being constrained by financial limitations. When you have multiple income streams, strong reserves, and a well-structured portfolio, you gain flexibility. You can choose when to invest, when to scale, and when to pause. This flexibility is one of the most valuable outcomes of mastering these strategies.

Another important concept is independence. By building your own system for income and financing, you reduce your reliance on traditional employment or restrictive lending criteria. You create a pathway where your business income and financial strategy work together to support your goals. This independence allows you to operate on your own terms.

Leverage remains a central component of your strategy. By using financing effectively, you can control larger assets and accelerate your growth. However, mastery involves using leverage responsibly. It means balancing growth with stability, ensuring that your cash flow remains positive, and managing risk effectively.

Another key element is adaptability. Markets change, lending guidelines evolve, and new opportunities emerge. Mastery requires staying informed and being willing to adjust your strategy as needed. This adaptability ensures that you can continue to thrive in different environments.

Long-term thinking is also essential. Every decision you make should be aligned with your overall vision. Whether you are acquiring a property, refinancing, or adjusting your strategy, each action should contribute to your long-term goals. This perspective allows you to build a cohesive and sustainable financial system.

Another important aspect of mastery is simplicity. While the strategies in this book may seem complex, the goal is to create a system that is easy to maintain and replicate. By simplifying your processes and focusing on key principles, you can operate more efficiently and with greater clarity.

Your network and team also play a critical role in your success. Surrounding yourself with knowledgeable professionals and like-minded individuals allows you to continue learning and growing. Collaboration and shared knowledge can open new opportunities and provide valuable insights.

As you move forward, you will begin to see the compounding effect of your efforts. Each property, each loan, and each strategic decision builds on the previous one. Over time, this creates a system that generates income, builds equity, and supports your lifestyle.

Another powerful concept is legacy. While this chapter focuses on mastery and freedom, it also connects to the long-term impact of your actions. The system you build today can continue to create value for years to come, providing opportunities and stability for future generations. Ultimately, this chapter is about stepping into a new level of confidence and capability. You are no longer just a participant in the system—you are a strategist who understands how to navigate and optimize it. This shift in perspective is what allows you to achieve true financial control.

Real-Life Math Example: Achieving Financial Freedom Through Strategic Execution

Let's walk through a comprehensive example that brings together all the concepts from this book and demonstrates how a borrower can achieve financial freedom through strategic execution. Imagine a borrower named Victor who owns a service-based business and has implemented the strategies outlined in this series.

Victor's business generates $700,000 in annual deposits. After excluding ineligible deposits, the lender determines that $650,000 is eligible revenue. Victor works with his CPA to prepare a profit and loss statement showing an expense ratio of 30%, resulting in a qualifying income of $455,000 annually, or approximately $37,916 per month.

Using a 45% debt-to-income ratio, Victor can qualify for monthly housing payments of approximately $17,062. He uses this capacity to build a portfolio of investment properties over time.

Victor acquires five properties, each generating $3,500 per

month in rental income. This results in a total rental income of $17,500 per month. After applying a 75% factor, the lender considers $13,125 as qualifying rental income.

Combined with his business income, Victor's total qualifying income reaches $51,041 per month. At this level, his borrowing capacity increases significantly, allowing him to continue expanding his portfolio.

Each property generates approximately $1,200 per month in net cash flow, resulting in a total of $6,000 per month. This income provides financial stability and supports Victor's lifestyle.

Victor also builds equity in his properties as they appreciate in value. After several years, each property increases in value by $150,000, resulting in a total equity gain of $750,000 across his portfolio.

Victor uses a cash-out refinance to access $300,000 in equity, which he reinvests into additional properties. This accelerates his growth and increases his income potential.

Over time, Victor's combined income from his business and rental properties reaches a level where his passive income covers his living expenses. This is the point where he achieves financial freedom—the ability to live without relying solely on

Risk management is also a critical component of long-term success. While leverage and growth are important, they must be balanced with stability and sustainability. Maintaining reserves, managing cash flow, and making informed decisions help protect your financial position and ensure that your growth is sustainable. This balance between growth and stability is what allows you to build lasting wealth.

As you continue your journey, it is important to remember that you are not alone. Working with experienced professionals—such as mortgage brokers, CPAs, and financial advisors—can provide valuable guidance and support. These relationships allow you to make informed decisions and navigate complex situations with confidence. Building a strong team is an investment in your success.

Another key takeaway is the importance of mindset. The strategies in this book are powerful, but they require a proactive and disciplined approach. By adopting a mindset of ownership and responsibility, you take control of your financial future. You move from reacting to circumstances to creating opportunities. This mindset is what allows you to fully utilize the tools and strategies you have learned.

As you reflect on everything you have learned, it is clear that business bank statement mortgage loans are more than just a financing option—they are a gateway to new possibilities. They provide access to opportunities that may not have been available through traditional methods. They allow you to leverage your business income, expand your investments, and build a system that supports your goals.

The journey does not end here. In many ways, this is just the beginning. The knowledge you have gained is meant to be applied, refined, and expanded upon. Each step you take, each decision you make, and each opportunity you pursue builds on the foundation you have created. Over time, this process leads to growth, stability, and financial independence.

You now have the tools to create your own path. You understand how to structure your income, optimize your financial profile, and navigate the lending process. You have the ability to turn your business into a powerful engine for opportunity. The next step is action—applying what you have learned and moving forward with confidence.

Financial success is not about luck—it is about understanding the system and using it to your advantage. You have taken the time to learn, to understand, and to prepare. Now it is time to execute. With discipline, consistency, and strategic thinking, you can achieve your goals and create a future that reflects your vision.

In the end, this book is about empowerment. It is about giving you the knowledge and confidence to take control of your financial journey. It is about showing you that there are multiple paths to success and that you have the ability to choose the one that works best for you. By applying these principles, you can build a system that supports your goals, creates opportunities, and provides long-term stability.

Your journey continues from here. Take what you have learned, apply it with intention, and continue to grow. The possibilities are not limited by the system—they are defined by how you choose to use it.

How to Get a Personalized Bank Statement Mortgage Review

If you found this book helpful, you may want to see how these strategies apply to your specific financial situation.

Bank statement mortgage lending is highly customized—your deposits, income patterns, expense ratios, credit profile, property type, and long-term goals all play a role in determining what you qualify for and how your loan should be structured.

Every borrower's situation is different. The way your income flows through your accounts, how your business operates, your credit history, the property you are purchasing or refinancing, and current lender guidelines all impact your options. The strategies and examples in this book are designed to teach you how bank statement mortgage loans work—but your actual qualifying income, loan amount, and loan structure can only be determined by analyzing your real financial profile.

If you would like a no-obligation Bank Statement Mortgage review, you can request one here:

Email: info@FinibiMortgage.com

A licensed mortgage broker will review your bank statements, income structure, credit profile, and goals, and explain what bank statement mortgage options may be available to you—including:

• 12-month and 24-month bank statement programs• Personal vs business bank statement qualification• Primary residence and investment property financing• Cash-out refinance and equity access strategies• Advanced structuring to maximize qualifying income

No cost. No pressure. No obligation.

Sincerely,

Joseph G. Correa

Finibi Mortgage Inc.

Licensed Mortgage Broker

About the Author

Joseph G. Correa is a licensed mortgage broker and the founder of Finibi Mortgage, a Florida-based brokerage specializing in bank statement mortgage loans, non-QM lending, and strategic real estate financing solutions for self-employed borrowers, entrepreneurs, and investors.

With more than two decades of experience in mortgage lending, underwriting, and deal structuring, Joseph has helped thousands of clients qualify for real estate using alternative income documentation, unlocking opportunities that traditional lending often restricts.

Unlike traditional loan officers who rely strictly on tax returns and W-2 income, Joseph's approach focuses on real cash flow, income structuring, and financial strategy. He believes that borrowers should not be limited by how income is reported on paper, but instead empowered by how income is actually earned and managed.

Joseph is widely recognized for his expertise in:

• Bank statement mortgage loans• Self-employed borrower financing• Non-QM and alternative income lending• Investment property and portfolio financing• Cash-out refinance and equity strategies• Advanced mortgage loan structuring

Through his education platform, Finibi Academy, Joseph has trained tens of thousands of students worldwide in mortgage strategy, real estate investing, credit optimization, and financial independence.

He created the **Bank Statement Mortgage Loan Mastery Series** to provide a clear, step-by-step roadmap for borrowers and professionals who want to qualify for real estate without relying on traditional income documentation.

His mission is simple: To help people use their real income—not just their tax returns—to qualify, invest, and build long-term wealth.

When he is not structuring loans or writing, Joseph works with clients across the United States to design customized mortgage strategies that align with their financial goals, income structure, and long-term investment plans.

The Bank Statement Mortgage Loan Mastery Series Roadmap

The Complete Guide to Qualifying for Real Estate Using Bank Statements Instead of Tax Returns

The purpose of the **Bank Statement Mortgage Loan Mastery Series** is to give borrowers, investors, and mortgage professionals the exact strategies used by lenders and underwriters—translated into simple, practical steps you can apply in real life.

This series takes you from beginner to advanced mastery of how to qualify, structure, and scale real estate financing using bank statements instead of traditional income.

Each book builds on the last. You are not just learning how to get approved—you are learning how to control your approvals.

Book 1 — Bank Statement Mortgage Loan Fundamentals

Learn how bank statement loans work, how income is calculated, and why tax returns are no longer required for many borrowers.

Book 2 — Personal Bank Statement Mortgage Loans

Learn how to qualify using personal accounts, structure deposits, and maximize usable income.

Book 3 — Business Bank Statement Mortgage Loans

Understand how lenders analyze business revenue, apply expense ratios, and use P&Ls.

Book 4 — Bank Statement Loans for Self-Employed Borrowers

Master how entrepreneurs qualify and structure income for approval.

Book 5 — Bank Statement Loans for Primary Residences

Learn how to buy or refinance your home using bank statement income.

Book 6 — Bank Statement Loans for Investment Properties

Discover how to scale rental portfolios using bank statement + DSCR strategies.

Book 7 — Jumbo Bank Statement Mortgage Loans

Learn how to finance high-value properties with advanced requirements and structuring.

Book 8 — Bank Statement Loan Refinancing & Cash-Out Strategies

Unlock equity, reduce payments, and reinvest capital using bank statement refinancing.

Book 9 — Bank Statement Loans with Credit Challenges

Learn how to qualify even with lower credit using compensating factors and strategy.

Book 10 — Advanced Bank Statement Mortgage Loan Structuring

Engineer approvals using deposits, expense ratios, and lender guidelines.

This series is designed to move you from understanding → execution → mastery.

By the end, you will not just know how to qualify—you will know how to structure deals like a professional.

Educational & Financial Disclaimer

The **Bank Statement Mortgage Loan Mastery Series** is intended for educational and informational purposes only.

This content is designed to help readers understand bank statement mortgage lending, real estate financing strategies, and income structuring concepts. It is not financial, legal, tax, or investment advice.

Joseph G. Correa and Live Stronger Faster are not acting as your personal financial advisor, attorney, accountant, or mortgage professional through this publication.

Mortgage guidelines, underwriting standards, interest rates, and loan programs vary by lender and may change at any time without notice.

All examples in this series are for illustration purposes only and do not guarantee approval or results.

Always consult with licensed professionals before making financial decisions.

Risk Disclosure

Bank statement mortgage lending and real estate investing involve risk.

Income fluctuations, interest rate changes, market conditions, and lender guidelines can all impact loan approval and financial outcomes.

Borrowing against real estate or using leverage increases both potential returns and risks.

Failure to repay a loan may result in foreclosure and loss of property.

Cash flow, rental income, and appreciation are not guaranteed.

All strategies in this series are educational and must be evaluated based on your individual financial situation.

You are solely responsible for your financial decisions.